THE CHEETAH

BEHAVIORAL SCIENCE SERIES

THE CHEETAH

*The Biology, Ecology, and Behavior
of an Endangered Species*

RANDALL L. EATON

BEHAVIORAL SCIENCE SERIES

**ROBERT E. KRIEGER PUBLISHING COMPANY
MALABAR, FLORIDA**

Original Edition   1974
Reprint   1982 , 1987

Printed and Published by
ROBERT E. KRIEGER PUBLISHING COMPANY, INC.
KRIEGER DRIVE
MALABAR, FLORIDA 32950

Printed in the United States of America

Library of Congress Cataloging in Publication Data

Eaton, Randall L., 1943-
   The cheetah: the biology, ecology, and behavior
of an endangered species.

   Reprint. Originally published: New York:
Van Nostrand Reinhold, c1974.
   Bibliography: p.
   Includes index.
   1. Cheetahs—Behavior. 2. Mammals—Behaviors.
I. Title.
QL737.C23E18   1982   599.74'428   81-18556
ISBN 0-89874-451-2   AACR2

10 9 8 7 6 5 4 3

599.759

To Erich and Katharine
for guidance and Frank
for making our ideas
become real.

BEHAVIORAL SCIENCE SERIES

The Van Nostrand Reinhold Behavioral Science Series will publish a broad range of books on animal and human behavior from an ethological perspective. Although presently observable behavior is the focus of this series, the development of behavior in individuals, as well as the evolutionary history in various species, will also be considered. It is felt that such an holistic approach is needed to come to a fuller understanding of behavior in general. This series is a contribution toward this goal.

Erich Klinghammer, Consulting Editor
Purdue University

Preface

My life with the cheetah began in 1966 and is still not ended. After a field study in East Africa and further study of cheetah behavior under semi-natural conditions, I am now faced with the task of putting my own observations and theories to work at World Wildlife Safari and Research Park where we are still studying and trying to breed this fine animal. It is a welcome but difficult challenge. Perhaps the most pressing task of the wildlife biologist is to apply biological and behavioral knowledge to achieve preservation of threatened species. My personal opinion is that many carnivores will become extinct in the wild before very long. For the difficult-to-breed species, such as the cheetah, their future may be limited to wildlife parks and zoos. We must work now to integrate information on the wild life of many species with their management in captivity, and hope thereby eventually to be in a position to reestablish many species in the wild.

I am pleased that the cheetah has become a fad in zoos around the world. I'm convinced that this growing interest and concern to propagate the species will succeed and will ensure the continued existence of cheetahs on our planet. It is equally encouraging that standards are being developed which will be required for American zoos planning cheetah breeding programs. This is an intelligent step forward in the captive preservation of vanishing animals. I should emphasize, however, the necessity for field studies of all wildlife, without which we are often only guessing about how best to manage a species, whether in the wild or in captivity.

Man will have to manage his entire heritage if he is to hold on to it. The quality of life around the globe is deteriorating daily. The more affluent societies must consider wildlife conservation as a top priority among all the other problems we now face. If we are successful in preventing the extinction of man, we may have left a world much less fit for human existence. The sight of a cheetah coursing prey, the mere thought that Siberian tigers still hunt the snow country are prime examples of what we stand to lose should we destroy the world and ourselves in the process. If man cannot marvel at anatomical machines more perfect than his creations, if he cannot ponder the significance of a sea urchin, he will cease being man the human, though he may survive as an animal. This then is the hardest question: do we care enough now that future generations will have these same things to appreciate?

To better express myself: ". . . into your hand are they delivered" (Genesis 9:2).

R. L. E.
Winston, Oregon

Acknowledgments

Financial support for this study came from an African Big Game Ecology and Behavior Graduate Research Fellowship awarded the author by the University of East Africa. Field transportation vehicles and photographic and safari equipment were provided by the University of East Africa and by Harshad and Dinesh Patel of Nairobi. My father, C. L. Eaton, generously assisted with the round-trip flight fare from Chicago to Nairobi.

Drs. Gordon H. Orians and Robert T. Paine of the Department of Zoology, University of Washington, Seattle, were helpful in outlining research ideas before the study began. Dr. Orians provided many helpful suggestions during and after the field work. Dr. Niko Tinbergen, Museum of Vertebrate Zoology, Oxford University, was inspiring and offered stimulating ideas while I visited Oxford en route to Nairobi.

Dr. Paul Leyhausen, Max Planck Institute at Wuppertal, Germany, has been informative in correspondence and discussions on behavior of the Felidae. Dr. Thane Riney, Forestry and Forest Products Division, Food and Agricultural Organization of the United Nations, Rome, Italy, offered constructive criticisms of the original research proposal. Dr. J. B. Foster, University College, Nairobi, was instrumental in acquainting me with the field study areas.

Dr. Fritz Walther at the University of Missouri, Columbia, made helpful criticisms on various aspects of my data and gave me access to his unpublished data on gazelle behavior which he gathered in East Africa.

Dr. Erich Klinghammer of Purdue University's Laboratory of Ethology, who was my major professor there, read and improved upon several phases of my cheetah research, part of which constituted a thesis for a Master of Science degree from Purdue.

Portions of the chapters on ecology and behavior were published in several scientific journals and I wish to thank the editors, especially Dr. Wolfgang Wickler, Editor, *Zeitschrift fur Tierpsychologie*, and Dr. Tony Peterlee, Editor, *Journal of Wildlife Management*, for their efforts in improving various drafts of manuscripts. Dr. Durward Allen read and made valuable suggestions on the manuscript.

I cannot thank Harshad Patel of Nairobi enough for being so kind as to accompany me in the field and photograph cheetahs. He has allowed me to use his superb photographs for illustration here. Mr. Patel uses the sale and exhibit of his photographic work to further the cause of wildlife conservation in East Africa.

Those who provided data on cheetah kills in Nairobi Park from their personal observations were: J. Thelinius, H. Patel, J. B. Foster, R. Casebeer, D. Kierney, L. Brown, A. Lasiewski, R. Bradley, J. P. S. Karmali, and M. Parry.

Following the field study, cheetahs living in semicaptive conditions were observed at Lion Country Safari, Laguna Hills, California. The 24 cheetahs came from South West Africa. Mr. Harry Shuster, President, and Mr. William York, Zoological Director and Chief Game Warden, both of Lion Country, were very helpful in a number of ways. They provided me with a vehicle and free access to the cheetahs during my stay. Several of the Game Wardens, especially Mr. S. Craig and Mr. D. Grubbs assisted me and were most helpful.

The Lion Country studies of cheetah social behavior were supported by a National Institute of Mental Health Neurobiology Fellowship, as part of my Ph.D. dissertation research at Purdue.

My wife, Katia Reye, has been and remains a constant inspiration in my work. She assisted me in the field, kindly typed the drafts for the book, and took many photographs.

Contents

THE CHEETAH

1 *Why, Where, and How*

SUBJECTIVE RESPONSES

Nearly two weeks passed until I finally saw a wild cheetah. Day after day I had ventured every road in Nairobi National Park, climbed each lookout, and sought the early morning report of the African Game Rangers who in pairs rode the trails on bikes before the park opened to the public. It seemed that all my previous experience of tracking deer and stalking geese in North America was to no avail here in this land where wildlife was supposed to be far more abundant, and less secretive.

Then, in the south end of the park, riding in a Land Rover with Bris Foster from the University College in Nairobi, I saw the "spotted sphinx." It was a male adult cheetah that ran at our approach in the car. He slipped away into the bush along the Athi River, and we lost sight of him. Judging from his flight response to our car this cheetah must have been in unusual haunts, a transient that showed fear in a far safer place than the Athi Plains into which he disappeared, and probably lived. That day was in October, 1966, and almost five years later, I learned that Nairobi Park may be expanded to encompass the Athi Plains and to be a closed ecosystem which will support the park's wildlife year round.

My concern and fascination with one animal in particular, the cheetah or hunting leopard, has largely directed my life for these five years. I

1

studied the cheetah in the wild and in captivity, and along with acquiring all the information I could on its ecology and behavior I have tried in many ways to see it conserved.

I have had to ask myself why—why does one man work with and for a particular species?

I should be honest and say that each man wants to be associated with something, and there are colleagues who call me a "cheetah man," just as my early mentor in wildlife was commonly referred to as "Mr. Duck." Perhaps I would take as much personal reward from being called a deer man, or a wood duck man had these animals taken more of my attention; however, I think not. The rewards are many and varied but intrinsically the cheetah fascinated me, more so than any animal I have ever observed. When Joy Adamson entitled her book about Pippa "The Spotted Sphinx," she could not have said it better for me. The cheetah gives me a feeling that it is a mystery no matter how much I learn about it. The cheetah seems to look through me rather than at me. Its concerns seem to be the honest and pure concerns of a quiet, graceful beast whose domain is its alone. It seems not aggressive and not shy but authoritatively indifferent. All the thousands of photographs I have taken still fail to impart or capture the essence that comes from looking into a live cheetah's eyes. They are totally captivating (see frontispiece).

These are subjective responses, and they are the motivation that keeps the wildlife student going. They are the rewards that drive one to keep pushing and learning in hopes of understanding an animal. It is a work of love. It is said that the ethologist differs from the comparative psychologist in that the former loves his animals. From what I have seen of the accomplishments in the two fields I would say that perhaps love is an important factor in the progress of science. But simply to love an animal is not to understand it, nor enough to conserve it. Instead we must know all we can of the hard facts of what an animal does, where it lives, and what it eats. We must attempt to collect objectively all the information possible or we do ourselves and the animal an injustice. Every animal is unique and if we are ever to understand nature fully we must know in what ways each animal differs from others. This is an immense task which may never be realized, especially since many animals are already extinct and the rate of extinction is ever increasing. We may not be able to stop extinction but we are certain to fail if we are ignorant of the endangered animal's needs and, moreover, unwise in our own lives.

While I shall not likely affect man's wisdom, I can hope to add to his knowledge which may in turn help the survival of one endangered species—the cheetah.

OBJECTIVES

One purpose of my field study was to make careful observations of cheetahs stalking and choosing their prey. In this way, it was hoped to determine the factors the cheetah uses as an indicator of an animal to be pursued, and whether the animals killed by the cheetah are other than a random sample of the total population. This information is important to determine whether or not certain classes of the prey animals are being culled from herds in the same way that wolves (*Canis lupus*) cull caribou (*Rangifer tarandus*) (*Murie, 1944*) and moose (*Alces alces*) (Mech, 1966, 1970) herds.

Aside from specific, ecological objectives, the fact that a species such as the cheetah is endangered but little-known is justification enough for studying its life in the wild and in captivity. Information on social behavior and various aspects of life history are important objectives in contributing to the comparative ethology of the Felidae, and carnivores in general. Behavior is how the animal interacts with its environment, and cannot be separated from ecology. Furthermore, our ecological understanding of a species is enhanced by knowing its ethology. The finest example from recent carnivore studies is the wolf. The wolf is elusive and difficult to observe for any continuous period in the wild. It was behavioral studies in captivity that revealed how wolves limit their numbers. Long-term observations of the pack at Brookfield Zoo (Woolpy, 1968) disclosed that very few individuals mate and consequently reproductive potential is greatly reduced. The higher-status individuals actively prevent the other pack members from mating, a case of social or psychological castration. The importance of both field and captive observation can not be underestimated in arriving at the total picture of any species. Information from the wild must be used to interpret captive behavior and vice-versa.

There has been great research interest in recent years in the social behavior of animals and humans (Etkin and Freedman, 1967). It is widely recognized that the study of captive primates provides information important to the understanding of human behavior, especially early experience and social organization. Recent field studies of primates (for example, Schaller, 1963) have provided important supplements to laboratory research.

In many respects, human behavior is qualitatively dissimilar to that of the other primates, apparently because man is the only primate that is a social hunter by nature. Human ecology and evolution have been different from the other primates for at least twelve million years (L.S.B. Leakey, pers. comm.). Recent scientific (Dart, 1964) and popular works (Ardrey, 1962; Lorenz, 1966) have argued that many human behaviorisms are unique among the primates chiefly as a result of his change from a forest-dwelling vegetarian to a plains-living "carnivore." Territorialism, intraspecific aggression, and several aspects of social behavior in man are very similar to these same behavior characteristics in the social hunting carnivores, for example the wolf and the lion. These behavioral similarities are to be expected since there would have been natural selection for similarly adaptive behavior in species occupying similar ecological niches. Students of social behavior in the wolf (for example Rabb, et al., 1967) have argued that in some respects the carnivores have as much to tell us about many aspects of human nature as do the primates. How ecology has affected the evolution of social organization in carnivores is germane to the understanding of our own species.

Wolf behavior has been studied in wild populations by Murie (1944) and Mech (1967, 1970). Knowledge of wolf social behavior has been expanded by studies in captivity (Schenkel, 1967; Rabb et al., 1967). The presence of cooperative behavior in hunting and in rearing and defending the young occurs in the wolf and in the wild hunting (or Cape) dog (*Lycaon pictus*) (Estes and Goddard, 1967). In both species the social group or pack is more than a family unit, consisting of unrelated but individually recognized members as well.

The cats, in general, do not live socially; however, as in the dog family, there exist varying degrees of social complexity. For example, the three big cats in East Africa constitute a continuum in which:
1. the leopard (*Panthera pardus*) is least social, with no adult social groups, and in which the adult female cares for the young by herself;
2. the cheetah has adult social groups of males, but the family unit is a single female and its young; and
3. the lion is most social. It has groups composed of all sex and age classes and the females share in the care of young.

(It should be mentioned that lion and cheetah exhibit wide variations of social organization that apparently reflect varying ecological conditions, for example in heavily forested bush and *miombo* woodland, lion prides are very small, often only two or three adults.) A long-term ethological objective to be met in the study of the big cats is our understanding of the evolution of social systems, that is, why they vary and what are the consequences of these variations.

My field work in Africa began on October 15, 1966, and was continued through February, 1967. The areas of investigation included several locations in Kenya and Northern Tanzania. Short trips were taken from the main study area, Nairobi National Park, to the Masai Amboseli Game Reserve, both in Kenya. Data were collected in Tanzania bordering the Masai Amboseli Game Reserve on two occasions. Also data were collected north of Nairobi National Park in the area between Maralel and Isiolo, in the North Frontier District of Kenya. This area would have been studied more intensively had it not been for the *Shifta* or Somali bandits who were causing havoc with their terrorist raids on the local natives. The area was closed to all visitors by the Kenya authorities, though unofficial entry was granted, along with a heavy rifle.

Although a good part of the wildlife research carried out in Africa is on the East African plains, this area is not really representative habitat on an African-wide basis. In fact the East African plains are a somewhat abnormal game region. Most of Africa's big game is found in regions that vary in character between the dry *miombo* woodland habitat and the wet savanna as in most of Uganda and the Congo parks. But the diversity of habitats and species is so great in East Africa that its atypical nature is counterbalanced. Biological field studies are more easily carried out there, and for studying cheetahs there is no better area since it contains one of the only sizable populations remaining in the entire world.

The lowland rain forest in Central and Western Africa does not extend as far east as Kenya. Kenya on the west and southwest is highland grassland and highland forest (Fig. 1–1). The vegetation type in Kenya is mostly affected by altitude and by rainfall. The rainfall areas are concentric around the Congo Basin (Dr. A. Agnew, pers. comm.). The Rift Valley creates a rain shadow area west of the valley, and it would be very dry except for the effect of Lake Victoria and the Congo Basin.

Kenya around Lake Rudolf is subdesert and in general is dry except for highlands and along the coast of the Indian Ocean. The major part of Kenya, the dry country, is *Acacia* and *Commiphora* savanna and grassland. It is usually not burned and is tsetse-fly (*Glossina pallidipes* and *G. swynnertoni*) country (Lambrecht, 1966). Talbot and Talbot (1963:18) say that the savanna or grassland is largely maintained by periodic fires, a common condition over the world.

Although the rainfall in most areas is up to 20 in. per year, this is misleading. The absolute rainfall is not as important to the vegetation and game as the variability of the rainfall. During my study the short rains were late—December—and the peak rains did not come until after the study was terminated, although they usually occur in October and March respectively.

Most of the data were collected in Nairobi National Park. Supporting data came mostly from the quite different Masai Amboseli Game Reserve. Nairobi National Park is rolling *Themeda triandra* grassland–*Acacia* savanna, and Masai Amboseli Game Reserve is flat, dryer *Acacia* savanna. Detailed maps of Nairobi Park (Fig. 1 –2) show contours, vegetation (Fig. 1–3), and landmarks important for further discussion.

Nairobi Park occupies an area of about 44 square miles, surrounded by a high fence on three sides. The south opens to the Athi River Plains and offers an area for game to enter and leave the park. Because of its

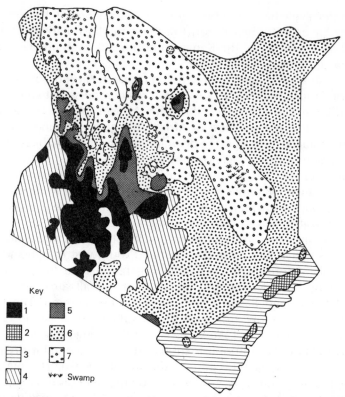

Key

1 5
2 6
3 7
4 ⱽⱽⱽ Swamp

Figure 1–1 Vegetation map of Kenya (after Stewart and Stewart, 1963). Key: 1 = highland grassland and highland forest; 2 = coastal forest; 3 = coastal grass–bush; 4 = grouped tree–grassland (including low tree–high grass); 5 = scattered tree–grassland and open grassland; 6 = desert grass–bush (dry bush with trees); 7 = desert scrub (and lava ridges, desert grass and shrub, and true desert).

yearround water supply from artificial dams it is a high concentration area for game, especially in the dry season. However, Nairobi Park is not a closed ecosystem because game move in and out and population densities fluctuate.

A dense forest lies in the extreme western border of Nairobi National Park and it is sectioned north to south by strips of riverine bush along water runoff areas. The vegetation is grassland plains interspersed with short 4–7 foot *Acacia drepanalobium.*

The soil type is a clay, commonly known as "black cotton." There is a hard pan about two feet under the ground surface and this may be responsible for the short growth of the *A. drepanalobium* by limiting the length of its single tap root system as suggested by Foster (1966).

Because cheetahs blend well or are completely hidden in tall grass, they

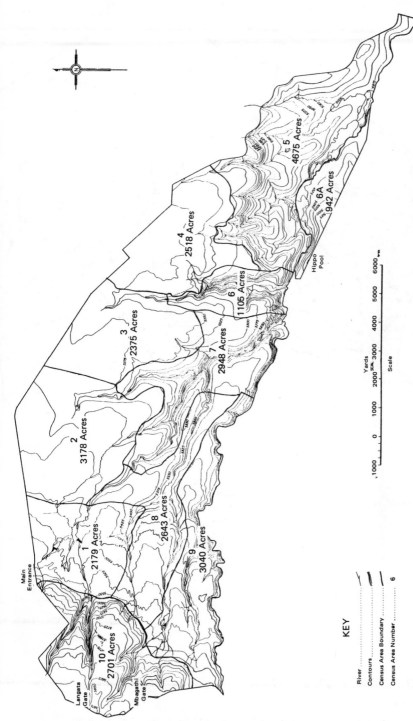

Figure 1–2 The northern and western areas of Nairobi National Park are at higher elevations. The water runoff is south to the Athi River which borders the park. Duplicate topographic maps were used to record daily movements of cheetahs.

NAIROBI   ROY

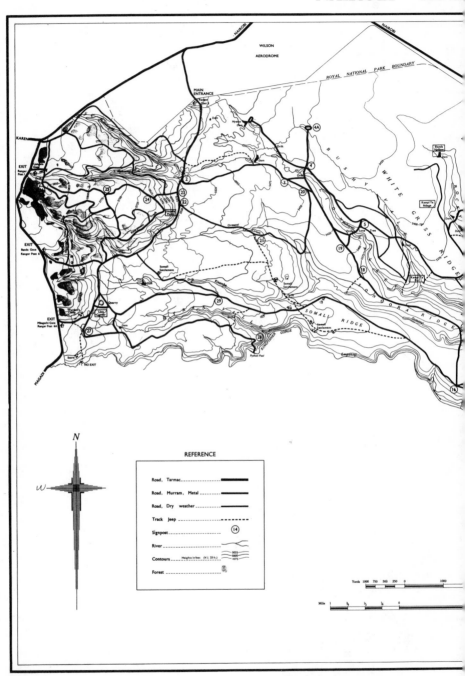

Figure 1–3   Nairobi National Park has a series of roads and landmarks that allow an observer access to most areas of the park for locating animals.

˥IONAI   PARK

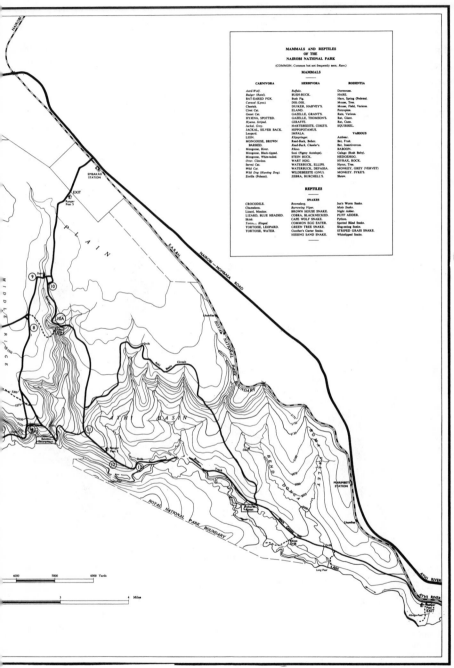

MAMMALS AND REPTILES
OF THE
NAIROBI NATIONAL PARK

(COMMON: Common but not frequently seen; *Rare*.)

MAMMALS

CARNIVORA	HERBIVORA	RODENTIA
Aard-Wolf.	Buffalo.	Dormouse.
Badger (Ratel).	BUSH-BUCK.	HARE.
BAT-EARED FOX.	Bush Pig.	Hare, Spring (Pedetes).
Caracal (Lynx).	DIK-DIK.	Mouse, Tree.
Cheetah.	DUIKER, HARVEY'S.	Mouse, Field, Various.
Civet Cat.	ELAND.	Porcupine.
Genet Cat.	GAZELLE, GRANT'S.	Rats, Various.
HYENA, SPOTTED.	GAZELLE, THOMSON'S.	Rat, Giant.
Hyena, Striped.	GIRAFFE.	Rat, Cane.
Jackal, Grey.	HARTEBEESTE, COKE'S.	SQUIRREL.
JACKAL, SILVER BACK.	HIPPOPOTAMUS.	
Leopard.	IMPALA.	**VARIOUS**
LION.	*Klipspringer.*	Antbear.
MONGOOSE, BROWN	Reed-Buck, Bohor.	Bat, Fruit.
BARRED.	*Reed-Buck, Chanler's.*	Bat, Insectivorous.
Mongoose, River.	*Rhino.*	BABOON.
Mongoose, Black-tipped.	Suni (Pigmy Antelope).	Galago (Bush Baby).
Mongoose, White-tailed.	STEIN BUCK.	HEDGEHOG.
Otter, Clawless.	WART HOG.	HYRAX, ROCK.
Serval Cat.	WATERBUCK, ELLIPS.	Hyrax, Tree.
Wild Cat.	WATERBUCK, DEFASSA.	MONKEY, GREY (VERVET)
Wild Dog (Hunting Dog).	WILDEBEESTE (GNU).	MONKEY, SYKE'S.
Zorilla (Polecat).	ZEBRA, BURCHELL'S.	Shrew.

REPTILES

SNAKES

CROCODILE.	*Boomslang.*	Jan's Worm Snake.
Chameleon.	*Burrowing Viper.*	Mole Snake.
Lizard, Monitor.	BROWN HOUSE SNAKE.	Night Adder.
LIZARD, BLUE HEADED.	COBRA, BLACKNECKED.	PUFF ADDER.
Skink.	CAPE WOLF SNAKE.	Python.
Torto... Hinged.	COMMON EGG EATER.	Spotted Blind Snake.
TORTOISE, LEOPARD.	GREEN TREE SNAKE.	Slug-eating Snake.
TORTOISE, WATER.	Gunther's Garter Snake.	STRIPED GRASS SNAKE.
	HISSING SAND SNAKE.	Whitelipped Snake.

Printed by 89 Fd. Svy. Sqd. R.E. and Survey of Kenya 3000/11/58
Compiled and drawn by Survey of Kenya from photogrammetric
mapping by Fairey Air Surveys Ltd. Sept. 1956

are difficult to locate in the field. In Masai Amboseli Game Reserve cheetahs were located more easily than in Nairobi Park, relative to the abundance of animals in each area. The Amboseli area is very flat and except for isolated islands of large *Acacia* is open and visibility is good (Fig. 1–4). Cheetahs were spotted by moving in a Land Rover, stopping, and then scanning with binoculars. A few short hills, volcanic in origin, were used as lookouts.

In Nairobi Park visibility is not as good because of short woody vegetation, high grass, and the rolling terrain (Fig. 1–5). The observation point (Fig. 1–3) is strategically located and high enough to overlook a good portion of the northern, flatter portion of the park. A 20 × spotting scope is provided for park visitors at the observation point and it proved invaluable on many occasions in spotting cheetahs. After the first three weeks of the study as much as five hours but never more were required to locate cheetahs either by scanning from the observation point or by driving through park roads using binoculars from a vehicle. Daily, game scouts are sent out in pairs on bicycles through all the roads of the park.

Figure 1–4 Cheetah standing near *Acacia drepanalobium* in Nairobi National Park. (Photo: H. Patel)

Figure 1–5 Waterbuck in Nairobi National Park. Note the rolling terrain and woody vegetation in the background. (Photo: R. L. Eaton)

Their function is to locate lions or any "attractive" species, for example rhinoceros, so that visitors can be told at the entrance where to look for game of their interest. The scouts' reports were useful only occasionally in finding cheetahs. When the cheetahs had been seen on a kill in the morning, they were usually located where they had been sighted.

Airplane flights were taken over the park to census cheetahs, but this system was less effective than ground observations. The park has monthly game censuses taken by qualified personnel, usually biologists working in the area who volunteer their time. These censuses are now being reported in the literature annually (Foster and Kearney, 1967; Foster and McLaughlin, 1968). The park is censused in different sections at the same time to eliminate duplications of counting. I participated in these counts and have used the data sheets for the months of my study. In my opinion the counts were accurately done. In some species it was difficult to sex accurately but general age classes, herd composition, and numbers were obtainable (Fig. 1–6).

Cheetahs were observed mostly from a vehicle since they showed little

Zone	1A	2	3A	1B	3B	4	5A	6A	7A	7B	8	9	A10	5-6	TOTAL
PRIMATES															
Baboons													1		1
Vervet Monkey												2			2
Sykes Monkey															
CARNIVORES															
Lion	1	1			4			4							10
Leopard		4													4
Cheetah															
Wild Dog															
Jackal	2	4													6
Bat-eared Fox		1													1
UNGULATES															
Grant's Gazelle	84	139	34	112	7	4	31	3	16	16	57	15	5	29	552
Thompson's Gazelle	139	106	18	37	21	1	5	14	20	1	50	5		6	423
Water Buck						3	16		35	11	9	5	5	18	102
Impala	9		47	23				16	60	76	60	124	164	6	585
Bush Buck			6	2	4	3		7	4						25
Wildebeest	64	67					73				41	28	22	40	335
Giraffe	14	8	1	3		2	2	2	7	4	8	7	16		74
Kongoni	107	290	90	62	93	31	45	58	109	49	69	96	12	149	1260
Eland	25						4		15		32	19	17		112
Reed Buck Bohors	1														1
Reed Buck Chandlers															
Duiker (Red)															
Steinbok															
Dik Dik															
Wart Hog	6	11	4	5	9	10	5			2	14	33	20	11	130
PERISSODACTYLA (Odd-toed)															
Rhino									1						1
Zebra	551	212	8	316	1	18	83			52	256	108	78		1664
Buffalo															
HYDRACOIDES															
Ostrich	1	16	8	6					10	9	41	8	6	2	126
Secretary Bird	1											4			5
Klipspringer								3							3
Totals	1005	859	216	566	139	72	264	107	277	220	637	454	346	261	5423

KENYA NATIONAL PARKS—GAME COUNT FOR OCTOBER, 1966

Figure 1–6 The game in Nairobi National Park are censused monthly by qualified personnel. (October census sheet courtesy of D. Kierney, Chief Warden, Nairobi National Park.)

fear of it. When possible, I stayed as far from the animals as accurate observation with field glasses permitted. Interference did occur when information was needed from a fresh kill since it was then necessary to approach within a few feet of the cheetah. Although it is impossible to be certain, I feel that my presence had very little effect on the behavior of cheetahs.

Cheetahs were followed around the clock from 5:30 a.m. to 7:00 p.m. When a group had been observed it could then be followed on successive days by intercepting them from the point where they were left on the preceding night (Fig. 1–7). When observations were needed on other groups they had to be located first and then followed. On several occasions two groups were close enough to be observed, and data were collected on both. On Sundays or holidays, when park visitation was high, cheetahs were sometimes bothered by numbers of cars crowding around them, and although they were easy to locate, their activities were hampered. Often, luckily, the lions were the prime attraction and they drew most of the tourists away from the cheetahs.

Sometimes when the terrain did not permit a vehicle, I followed cheetahs on foot and found that I did not frighten them as long as I remained well behind and moved slowly. Only once did a cheetah approach me. I was watching a group from the top of a small hill. I was lying on my stomach looking through binoculars and one of the five cheetahs had backtracked, gone around the hill, and was stalking me when I saw him about twenty yards away. Once I looked at the cheetah he remained still, watching me. After a few minutes I stood up and faced the cheetah. He suddenly stood up and returned my stare and we both stood motionless until I walked off the hill toward my car. Then the cheetah walked up the hill alternating his visual orientation from me to the spot where I had lain. Once at the spot he stopped and smelled the ground intensively while keeping his eyes on me. After two minutes of inspection he "chirped" in the direction of his family and slowly walked back to them.

Data were collected from many sources including park records, individuals' sightings and descriptions, and photographs of cheetahs, and of course my own observations.

In the field, all behavior and activities were recorded in field notebooks. In the evening, notes were rewritten and duplicate copies were kept in separate places to avoid loss or damage. Notation was made of wind direction and velocity, percentage of cloud cover, precipitation, and temperature. Duplicate contour maps were used to mark daily movements of cheetahs and locations of particular behavior (Fig. 1–2).

A portable tape recorder was used to take verbal notes when behavioral sequences occurred rapidly. A parabola was also used with the micro-

Figure 1-7 Mother and cubs bed down at dusk but remain wary of predators. (Photo: H. Patel)

phone to record cheetah vocalizations. Vocalizations were played back to captive cheetahs in the World Wildlife Foundation Animal Orphanage at Nairobi Park to observe their reactions.

Photography was initially important in identifying cheetahs. Pictures of the left side of the face were carried in the field to identify individual animals by their different spot patterns. When there was doubt as to an individual cheetah's identity, it was carefully approached and photographed with a telephoto lens. In time cheetahs became recognizable upon sight without reference to the photo file. Body size and shape, color of fur, and amount of white on the tip of the tail were all valuable cues.

Photography was vital for the recording of behavior for further analysis. The periodic assistance in the field of Mr. Harshad Patel of Nairobi, an expert photographer facilitated this phase of work.

It was important to be able to judge accurately distances between cheetahs and prey, distances cheetahs chased prey, etc. For this purpose I used a 200-ft field survey tape either to measure directly certain distances or to check estimates. While active in a different type of vegetational cover, measurements were taken more frequently since it took a while to adjust perceptually to the different terrain or cover.

The data on social behavior were, for the most part, collected at Lion Country Safari, a private-enterprise wildlife park (Eaton, 1970a, b) and recently at World Wildlife Safari and Research Park, Winston, Oregon. The California Lion Country Safari is located south of Los Angeles at Laguna Hills. The preserve area is about 150 acres with a winding tarmack road that moves through six respective sections. Two sections contain African ungulates, three have lion prides, and the last section has cheetahs. Tourists safari through Lion Country in their automobiles, observing and photographing the wildlife, usually at close range.

The 24 cheetahs, world's largest collection, all came from South West Africa. They roam free within their 3.5-acre compound, and are not closed up at night. The section is surrounded by 15 ft chain link fence. There is a sliding gate at the entrance operated by a game guard in a tower. The exit consists of a double row of fence with two gates manned by wardens to maintain complete security. At World Wildlife Safari, six (2:4) cheetahs from South West Africa are kept in a seven-acre compound, subdivided into three areas. The compound is separated from the drive-through park to minimize disturbance and maximize breeding.

Many of the same observational techniques were employed in the captive phase of the research; however, sound recordings were played back to the cheetahs, and their responses observed. More time was spent on foot at Lion Country Safari, but at World Wildlife Safari observation was carried out from a distance. At Lion Country cheetahs charged frequently at first but later ignored me. I was able to approach, sit, and observe within 30 ft except at feeding. Frequently, I stood on top of a jeep to take movies of feeding behavior and the fighting associated with feeding. Carcasses of sheep, horses, and a few African ungulates that died in the preserve were thrown into the cheetah section to observe competitive interactions at a single carcass.

Evening observations during moonlit nights were made at Lion Country Safari and I slept just outside the perimeter fence on many dark evenings to record activity levels, being awakened by the cheetahs' vocalizations.

The various experiments and the procedures employed are described throughout the text.

I took no movies in Africa, but did at Lion Country and World Wildlife Safari. The movies proved most valuable in analyzing behavior patterns and interactions in detail.

2 The Cheetah

EVOLUTION

The earliest known fossil records of cheetah are from the Olduvai I bed, which includes many lower Pleistocene fauna fossils (Hopwood, 1951). The "Larousse Encyclopedia of Animal Life" (1967) says that since there are no fossil remains of cheetah in Africa, this negative evidence points to an Asian origin. The cheetah has evolved independently from the other big African cats, the *Panthera* group. The lion and leopard and the tiger in Asia evolved more recently in response to the increase in size and kinds of larger prey animals. The *Panthera* cats are distinguished by a difference in the hyoid bone apparatus which permits roaring. The cheetah, unlike these other big cats, does not roar; however the cheetah purrs similar to the *Felis* cats, for example the housecat and cougar.

TAXONOMY

Acinonyx jubatus was used as the cheetah's scientific name by Schreber in 1776; *Felis jubata* was used by Exrleben in 1777 (Shortridge, 1963:104). The taxonomy of the cat family has been in a state of flux. From up-to-date classifications by many authors, Denis (1964:133–136) produced a checklist of the family Felidae. This classification shows that of 36 distinct species, excluding varieties and subspecies, 30 are in the genus *Felis*, 5 in *Panthera*, and 1 in *Acinonyx*. Although some authors used *Felis* for the cheetah as late as 1884 (Sterndale, 1884:200), in general *Acinonyx* is in widest usage (Shortridge, 1934:104; Burton, 1962:187; Roberts, 1951:181; and others). A few authors have used generic names other than *Felis* or *Acinonyx*. Roberts (1951:181) lists the following: *Cynofelis* by Lesson, 1842; *Guepardus* by Duvernoy, 1834; *Geuparda* by Layard, 1861; and *Cynailurus* by Elliot, 1883. Flower and Lydekker (1891:523) also used *Cynailurus*.

There have been many species, subspecies, and races described for the cheetah. Denis (1964:136) states that there are two races, in Africa and Iran, but does not say what their differences are. Several subspecies have been described: a South African cheetah, *A. jubatus jubatus* (Schreber); three East African cheetahs, *A. jubatus ngorongorensis* (Hilzheimer), *A. j. velox* (Heller), and *A. j. rainey* (Heller); a Sudan subspecies, *A. j. soemmeringii* (Fitzinger); a Senegal or North African subspecies, *A. j. hecki* (Hilzheimer); an Indian subspecies, *A. j. venaticus;* and *A. j. raddei* (Hilzheimer), a Turkestan subspecies.

Only a second African species, the King or Cooper's cheetah, *A. rex* Pocock, is listed by Harper (1945:286). There can be little doubt that much of the subspeciation, as the three in East Africa, is artificial classification. Isolated populations, such as those formerly found in India, have been geographically isolated long enough to obtain distinct physical characteristics. The King (Rex) cheetah or *A. rex* appears to be a population in which all phenotypic features, according to Roberts (1951:182), are the same as *A. jubatus* except for coloration and pattern of the fur (Fig. 2–1). All other cheetah populations show only slight variation in markings. Sightings and specimens of Rex have come from a small local region of Southern Rhodesia, northwest of Salisbury. This type has probably arisen via a single mutation, and the population probably should not be given species status unless it can be demonstrated that there has been genetic isolation from the nonmutant form. The Rex cheetah may now be extinct, since none have been seen for several years.

The name cheetah is derived apparently from the Hindi language in India that uses the word "chita," which means spotted one. Early writers in India use "chita" and "cheeta" (Flower and Lydekker, 1891:523). "Hunting leopard" is also in common usage today (Burton, 1962:187; Sterndale, 1884:200; Flower and Lydekker, 1891:523; Denis, 1964:136; Shortridge, 1934:104; Crandall, 1964:396; and others). Additional names in various continental languages are *guepard,* French; *Gepard,* German; *gheparde,* Italian, and *onza,* Spanish. Roberts (1951:181) and Shortridge (1934:104) list numerous native words for the cheetah. In Swahili, which was used often in my field study to question natives about cheetah whereabouts,

Figure 2–1 King cheetah from the Siki Reserve in Rhodesia. Mounted specimen in the Natal Museum.

"enduma" is the name. The Masai call the cheetah "nginyarasho." The Kikamba use the name "munyongoro," and there probably are many more local usages.

DISTRIBUTION

In the writings of Marco Polo (Wendt, 1959:56–57) cheetah were described and apparently numbered in the hundreds as hunting pets of the Mongol rulers. It can not be certain that cheetah were native in the Far East, since they may have been imported by the Mongols from areas further west. Crandall (1964:396) includes much of Africa, Arabia, Persia, and India as original cheetah range. Others include the arid and semiarid regions of South, East, and North Africa as well as less arid areas in India, Russian Turkestan, Syria, Palestine, and Arabia. In 1891, Flower and Lydekker (523) gave its distribution as throughout Africa and southwestern parts of Asia as far as southern India. Sterndale (1884:200) gave central and southern India, and in the northwest from Kandeish to the Punjab as its Indian range, and wide distribution through Syria, Arabia, Asia Minor, and all of Africa.

Its Asian range is greatly reduced and the same pattern seems to be developing in Africa. MacDonald (1966:70) says, ". . . but now they have almost disappeared from those lands [India and Near Eastern countries] and are plentiful only in Africa." The cheetah is extinct in India and is reported to be very rare in Pakistan, Afghanistan, and Russia.

The history of the cheetah in Asia is one of decline and no recovery. The most recent sighting in India was 1951. Iraq, 1928 was the last sighting and until recently remnant populations persisted in Saudi Arabia, Oman, and perhaps Asian Russia. However, the cheetah is increasing now in north-west Iran, a tribute to the excellent game department there (Firouz, 1971; F. Harrington, pers. comm.).

In South West Africa the cheetah had a widely scattered range throughout the eastern sand-veld regions and apparently were increasing in Buchuanaland in 1934 (Shortridge, 1934:105). In southern Africa the cheetah has disappeared from the Cape Province, the Orange Free State, Natal, and the southern Transvaal. Thirty years ago they were rare throughout Southern Rhodesia, sparse in Northern Rhodesia (Zambia today), and rare in Nyasaland (Shortridge, 1934:105–106; Roberts, 1951:182). Cheetah occur throughout East Africa, north through Somalia, Ethiopia, and Arabia west to Nigeria (Petrides, 1965), but the only areas of real abundance outside of East Africa were probably Somalia and Ethiopia and the Somalia population has declined very recently due to no protection there. The East African countries Uganda, Kenya, and Tanzania until recent times had sizable populations (Fig. 2–2) (Graham and Parker, 1965). For Kenya, Stewart and Stewart (1963:6) give the present range of the cheetah based on sightings from many sources (Fig. 2–3).

A recent study (N. Myers, pers. comm.) indicates that the largest cheetah population in the world is in South West Africa, and that the population in East Africa is second largest.

DESCRIPTION

Meinertzhagen (1938) gives the weights of four freshly killed males in Kenya as from 127 to 143 pounds and that of a single female as 139 pounds. Shortridge (1939:109) lists two specimens weighing 136.5 pounds and 90 pounds, sex of the animals not given. Roberts (1951:181–182) gives weights of specimens from near Kruger National Park, males weighing 130, 110, and 108 pounds and a female weighing 127 pounds. Bourliere (1963) gives an estimate of 120–140 pounds for cheetah.

Letting Meinertzhagen's four male weights average 135 pounds, the average of 11 cheetah is 125.5 pounds. All known males average about 127 pounds, known females average 133 pounds in weight. This sample is entirely too small to generalize on male-female weight comparisons, but it

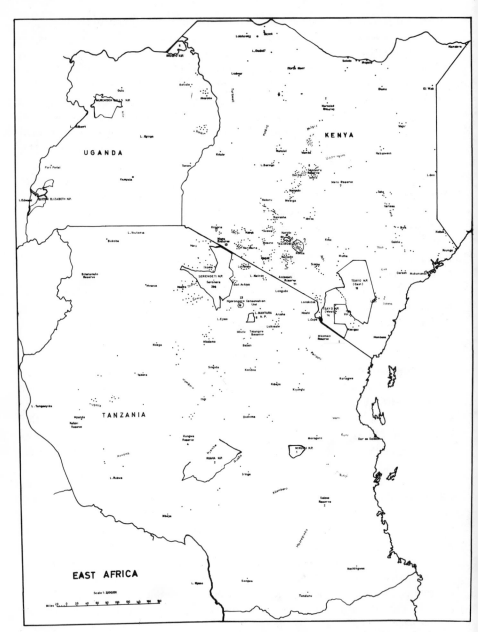

Figure 2–2 The sightings of cheetahs in East Africa between 1955 and 1964. Each dot represents one sighting; the numbers are cheetahs observed in respective reserves. (From Graham and Parker, 1965. Reproduced with permission.)

does give some idea of average adult weight. The Lion Country Safari and the San Pasqual Wild Animal Park's 34 cheetahs were all taken from the wild in South West Africa. Weights range from about 80 pounds for the smallest female at two years age, to 110 pounds for the largest males. Average adult weight was about 100 pounds.

Shoulder heights are recorded by Shortridge (1934:104) as 2 ft 11 in. for a large specimen; 2 ft 6 in. to 3 ft for several cheetah (exact number not given); and 2 ft 5 in. to 2 ft 7 in. as the range by Lydekker. Stevenson-Hamilton (1947:348) gives 2 ft 6 in., 2 ft 7 in., and 2 ft 8 in. for three males.

Total length measurements (nose to tip of tail) are given below. Shortridge (1934:109–110) lists the total length of the three largest specimens recorded by Rowland Ward Safari Company; the fourth one is from a female, and the last two are unidentified as to sex:

1. 7 ft 9 in., Kenya
2. 7 ft 3 ¼ in., North West Rhodesia
3. 7 ft 2 ½ in., North West Rhodesia
4. 6 ft 3 in., Kenya
5. 6 ft 8 in., Eastern Transvaal
6. 7 ft 7 in., Eastern Transvaal

Stevenson-Hamilton (1947:348) gives 6 ft 11 in., 6 ft 8 in., and 6 ft 4 in. for the total length of three males in South Africa. Roberts (1951:181–182) gives as total lengths of unsexed cheetahs 6 ft 7 in. (straight) and 6 ft 10 in. (on curves).

These total length measurements may not be meaningful. It is not known if they were measured properly. One specimen recorded by Roberts showed there is quite a difference in measuring straight or along body curvations.

Stevenson-Hamilton (1947:348) lists body and tail measurements (along with total length) and they are respectively: 52 in., 31 in., 51 in., 30 in.; and 47 in., 29 in. Roberts (1951:182) treats *A. rex* separately, and gives body and tail measurements for it from dry skins: 50 in., 30 in.; and 53 in., 30 in. Although these measurements correspond with Roberts' measurements of *A. jubatus* from whole carcasses, dry skin measurements are meaningless.

Skull measurements provided by Roberts (1947:564) indicate that cheetah in South Africa have the same measurements as those in East Africa. This indicates taxonomic similarity of widely separated populations and supports a "clumping" view of cheetah taxonomy. However, captive cheetahs from East Africa are decidedly less rangy than cheetahs from South West Africa. Also discernible is the darker pelage of South West African cheetahs.

The dentition of the cheetah differs from other *Felidae* by the inner

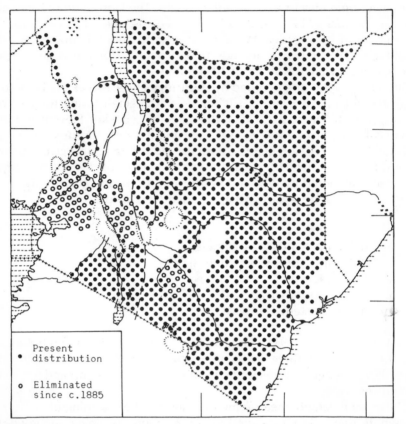

Figure 2–3 The distribution of the cheetah in Kenya. (From Stewart and Stewart, 1963.)

tubercle of the upper carnassial, although supported by a distinct root, it has no salient cusp (Flower and Lydekker, 1891:523).

GENERAL APPEARANCE

The cheetah's exaggerated cursorial proportions are well known and apparent to any observer (Fig. 2–4). General color would have to be considered yellow or tan but individuals vary as to the degree of color, some being light and others dark. They are covered everywhere with round black spots about half an inch in diameter. The neck and shoulders have longer thin hair that forms a short mane. The face, too, is covered with small spots and a long black line from the inside of the eye to the mouth. The ear is small and round with a black patch on the back side, which is apparently an adaptation similar to that found in many animals that serves as a pair of "fake" or mimic eyes. It has not been tested, but hypothetically a predator approaching from the rear of the cheetah might perceive the cheetah as being aware, and therefore should not attack.

The tail is long, and in adults, white on the tip. Ewer (1971) believes that the tip of the tail helps cubs follow the mother through high grass. The eyes are extremely large with golden or brown irises. The cheetah's feet are unusual for *Felidae,* being very dog-like with partially nonretractile claws (Fig. 2–5 and 2–6). The claws, according to Shortridge (1891:523) are less retractile because of feebler development of the elastic ligaments. Adamson (1969) noted that even newborn cubs could not retract claws. The head is small and round.

Besides a skeletal framework that is, like the greyhound's, highly adapted for speed, the cheetah has relatively large nasal passages for heavy breathing, large bronchi and lungs, relatively large heart and adrenals, and highly muscular arteries. The long tail functions to maintain balance at high speeds, and the nonretractile claws, which become blunt and short with wear, serve for good traction and quick turns.

Estimates of maximum speed in the cheetah vary from 60 miles per hour to nearly 80 miles per hour. The slower speeds have been made in artificial situations, for example on a dog racing track with a hare as bait.

Figure 2–4 The cheetah's anatomy is highly specialized for speed. (Photo: H. Patel.)

Figure 2–5 Relaxed cheetah exhibits its partially nonretractile claws. (Photo: R. L. Eaton.)

Observations in the wild that employed stop watches and measurements of distances covered should more accurately assess top speeds. One such record shows that a cheetah covered more than 700 yards in 20 seconds, which is a rate of more than 71 miles per hour (Bourliere, 1954:6–7). My own observations do not corroborate Bourliere's. A cheetah seldom runs at top speed for more than 200–300 yards. Moreover, in Florida a captive cheetah was accurately clocked at 71 miles per hour top speed (K. Sevrin, pers. comm.) for a short distance.

Professor Hildebrand of the University of California, Davis, has intensively studied the functional anatomy of the cheetah. His researches have disclosed the interesting hypothesis that, if the legs were discounted entirely, the movements of the body would propel the cheetah forward at a speed of five miles per hour. By using slow motion films, Hildebrand has been able to stop, analyze, and diagram the locomotory movements, showing the progression of each foot during high-speed running.

HABITAT PREFERENCE

There is some question as to what is the habitat preference of the cheetah. It is too often assumed by popular writers that the cheetah is found only in the open grassland. I think this stems from the fact that photographers and hunters have most often seen cheetah only in the very open grasslands, especially in northwestern Tanzania and southeastern Kenya. Burton (1962:187) gives "open grassland or scrub" as cheetah habitat. Denis (1964:40) says they are adapted to savanna or open grassland. In India, cheetahs were recorded in very dense forest regions. In South Africa, Stevenson-Hamilton (1947:196) describes cheetah as found in open or lightly forested grass country and adds his opinion that thick bush is detrimental to its method of securing prey. Shortridge (1934:106) met cheetah in South West Africa on stony ridges as well as in the sand veld and less often in country clothed with dense bush or thick dry forest montane moorland or swamp. The species would appear to occupy a wide range of habitat from near desert through open grassland to thick bush.

The Cheetah Survey (Graham and Parker, 1965:11) did not disclose many sightings in the extensive tracts of Brachystegia or *miombo* woodland that make up large areas of Tanzania and much of Africa. In addition, the survey showed no sightings in the extensive "long grass" areas of Uganda. Lamprey (1963:65) divides the habitat in the Tarangire Game Reserve into three types: grass, open woodland, and dense woodland. He shows the cheetah (Fig. 2–7) as preferring mostly grassland with some use of open woodland. My observations show that cheetah frequent open woodland

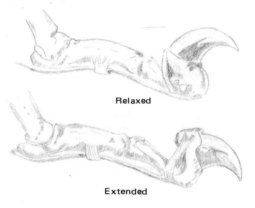

Relaxed

Extended

Figure 2–6   Cat claws. When not in use, the claw-bearing joint of each toe is folded back over the preceding joint and held in place by a ligament. In this position it is encased in a sheath of skin for further protection. When the animal extends its paw to strike, a tendon attached to each toe pulls the joint forward and bares the claws for instant use. The cheetah differs from other cats in the absence of claw sheaths; the blunt claws always remain exposed and extended.

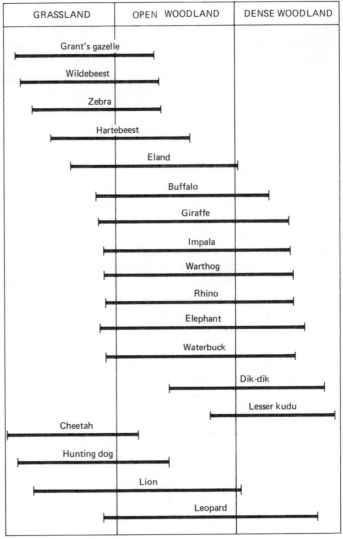

Figure 2–7 The ecological separation of mammals shown by Lamprey (1963:65) for Tarangire Game Reserve, Tanganyika. (Reproduced with permission.)

more often than shown by Lamprey, in fact they occasionally use dense woodland in hunting (Fig. 2–8). Warren Garst (pers. comm.) filmed cheetahs in Rhodesia in *miombo* woodland habitat nearly devoid of open space.

Only observations from following animals continually would reveal the total habitat visitation of the species. Cheetah in open or dense woodland are naturally less visible and this factor, I think, has biased earlier interpretations of their habitat. Of course, my observations do not represent the habitat visitation of all cheetah everywhere and in fact they may be biased due to special habitat preferences of the local populations I observed. Still, the fact that any local population, as in Nairobi National Park, frequents open woodland and savanna and even uses dense woodland expands the habitat preference for the species as a whole and may indicate that other populations behave similarly.

Adamson (1969) noted the frequent use of trees as lookouts in her tame, wild-living cheetahs in Kenya. She deduced that man had driven the cheetah out of the open plains into wooded areas thus indirectly leading to use of trees and climbing. While mortality from man is probably higher in open areas, I am confident that cheetahs have always occupied the less open, wooded areas. Cheetahs climb and seek out high lookouts in open areas as well.

ABUNDANCE

The only area in the cheetah's distribution for which information is available concerning density and abundance is East Africa. Graham and Parker (1965) and Graham (1966) analyzed data from the East African Cheetah Survey. The density was estimated at 1 animal per 18 square miles for the Narok District in Kenya and surrounding areas, based on 12 animals in the Mara triangle of 216 square miles. For the Tarangire Game Reserve, Tanzania, and surrounding country the estimate of density was 1 animal to 170 square miles; however, this is based on transect counts of two square miles of Tarangire between 1958 and 1961, a crude approximation to say the least!

The only area for which estimates of density were more than crude approximations is Nairobi National Park and the Serengeti Area. The

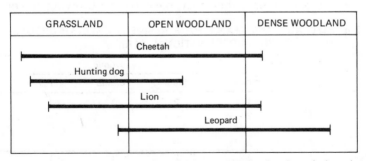

GRASSLAND	OPEN WOODLAND	DENSE WOODLAND
	Cheetah	
Hunting dog		
	Lion	
	Leopard	

Figure 2–8 In Nairobi National Park the "niche" is wider for the cheetah than shown by censuses in the Tarangire Game Reserve by Lamprey (1963).

Cheetah Survey (Graham and Parker 1965:9–10) gives an estimate based on numerous reliable observations by Dr. R. Schenkel, Zoologist, and D. Kierney, Chief Game Warden, Nairobi National Park. These two competent observers agreed on the presence of 12–14 animals consisting of 2–4 single adults, 4 male adults, and 1 adult with 5 young. The density for the park based on the 1963–64 period of observations by Schenkel and Kierney was 12–14 animals in 44 square miles or 1 animal to 3–4 square miles.

In all fairness, it should be stated that these men probably had good knowledge of some groups of cheetah in the park, but from my own experience I can say that Kierney was not aware of some of the resident cheetah while I was working there. Of course some of the occasional sightings not recognized by Schenkel and Kierney could have been nonresident cheetah that came in from outside the park for a short time only. Still, there were recorded a group of 2, a group of 3, and a group of 2 adults with 3 young. If these cheetah were also residents of the park, then the maximum number of cheetah in the park would have been almost twice as large—22–24 animals or a density of 1 animal to about every 2 square miles. The inclusion of these animals in the original estimate gives a revised estimate very much like the density and abundance of cheetah present during my study.

I observed a total of 20 different cheetah in Nairobi National Park. Of these 20 animals, I considered 15 to be residents (Table 2–1), that is, cheetahs whose home range included some or all of the park. One group, a female adult with three young and a single adult were observed in the park only twice and once respectively, and were considered nonresidents.

That the seldom observed cheetah were nonresidents of the park is supported by the fact that they showed greater fear of vehicles and were "jittery" in general. Assuming that there were at least 15 resident cheetahs, my data show a density in the park of 1 animal to nearly 3 square miles. Since I observed more resident cheetah but fewer single adults than Schenkel and Kierney, and since they had no means of identifying animals other than by group size, they may have been observing fewer single

TABLE 2-1 SIZE, AGE, AND SEX OF FOUR RESIDENT CHEETAH GROUPS OBSERVED IN NAIROBI NATIONAL PARK

| Group | Adult | | Juvenile | | | Total |
	Male	Female	Male	Female	?	
#1	—	1	2	1	1	5[a]
#2	3	2	—	—	—	5
#3	2	—	—	—	—	2
#4	2	1	—	—	—	3
Totals	7	4	2	1	1	15

[a] Two of the four cubs were lost on December 15, presumably by lion predation.

adults than they realized. After I left Nairobi Park, a second researcher, McLaughlin, studied cheetahs. He found about 20 cheetahs that resided in the park.

In the Masai Amboseli Game Reserve, which is thought to be a good cheetah sanctuary, I observed a total of 8 cheetahs. The reserve is 1300 square miles and I was not able to locate and record individuals throughout the entire area. It is difficult for a researcher to determine where in the reserve he is. There are no signs, permanent roads, or fences partly due to its management for the government by the Masai people. What is more, the area is fast losing any value as a reserve due to extreme competition between Masai cattle and game for food and water. Schaller (1970) earlier estimated that the average density of cheetah in the Serengeti was 1 per 100 square miles. He felt population was declining there for unknown reasons, but more recently (1972) has stated that the population appears to be holding its own. Schaller (1972) guesses that there are about 200–250 cheetah in the Serengeti ecological unit, a density of less than one cheetah per 40 square miles.

The total estimate for East Africa based on 1225 sightings of 2785 cheetah was 1932–1950 different animals in 1965. The accuracy of cheetah estimates will vary with the number of observers in the area, the terrain, and vegetation, and the experience of the observers. If about 2000 different animals were actually seen, then there probably were many more in highly unvisited areas such as in Northern Kenya. For example, no cheetah were observed in Rodgers Valley in the North Frontier District of Kenya according to the Cheetah Survey's map (Fig. 2–2). Yet, reliable observers recorded 15 different cheetah in Rodgers Valley in one trip. The North Frontier District (N.F.D.) has yielded very high numbers of observations in its few inhabited areas. These facts imply that the estimate given by the Cheetah Survey probably falls very short of the actual numbers of cheetah in some areas, and for the whole of East Africa was probably too low in 1965.

Earlier visitors, for example Bill York, frequently saw from a dozen to 20 or more cheetahs in a small area of southern Sudan near the Illemi triangle. In recent times reports have indicated fewer or no cheetahs there. We shall await the results of Norman Myers' current study of cheetahs to reevaluate its status in several countries.

REPRODUCTIVE BIOLOGY

With any threatened species, such as the cheetah, it is important to have information on reproductive biology as an aid in breeding them in captivity so that individuals will not be removed from existing populations. Further, population trends can be evaluated from analysis of reproductive organs as well as composition of a population by sex and age classes. Captive animals as opposed to individuals from wild populations can be used to restock areas formerly occupied, and this is now being tried in South Africa. Table 2-2 includes measurements and estimates of gestation periods in cheetahs. There are few data on wild cheetahs, but most observations indicate a 90–95 day gestation period.

TABLE 2-2   ESTIMATES AND MEASUREMENTS OF GESTATION
            IN CHEETAHS

Source	Wild or Zoo Cheetahs	Gestation, Days (No. Litters)
Asdell (1964)	zoo	95
Ulmer (1957)	zoo	92
Wilhelm, in Shortridge (1934)	wild	90
Kenneth (1943) in Asdell (1964)	zoo	95
Adamson (1969)	semi-wild	90 (3)
Herdman (1972)	semi-captive	92–95 (2)
Florio and Spinelli (1968)	zoo	86–90

Crandall (1964:397) describes a female in captivity that gave birth on March 24, 1956, and again on April 25, 1957. Assuming that gestation was about 90 days, this female was impregnated 10 months following parturition, an anestrous period of 13 months. Graham and Parker (1965:18) describe an adult female and a three-fourths grown male that were approached by an adult male. The adult male kept driving off the young male and kept very close to the female. In Nairobi Park, J. B. Foster (pers. comm.) observed a group of adult male cheetahs approach and mate with a female that was accompanied by cubs estimated to be one-half to three-fourths grown. Since females raise their young in isolation from other adults until the cubs reach sexual maturity at 14–16 months, the three-fourths grown male was probably the female's cub, apparently about 10 months old. The cubs observed by Foster were also roughly 10 months old. In both cases anestrus was about 13 months. Sterndale (1884:203) observed a female with two older cubs accompanied by an adult male. The female was probably in estrus, but from Sterndale's description it is not possible to determine the age of the cubs. Spinelli and Spinelli (1968) describe a captive female that came into heat four months after birth of a litter.

In Nairobi Park I observed one female with cubs from the time the cubs were 5½–10 months old. During this period adult males did not approach the family group. Foster and McLaughlin (1968) observed this same female after I left Africa. Her cubs left her when they were 15 months of age and in another 3–4 months she gave birth again, a period of 15–16 months between birth and conception. Adamson's (1969) semiwild cheetah, Pippa, gave birth to her first litter which was lost at six weeks of age. The female mated again within two weeks and about three months later gave birth to four cubs. Pippa mated again when these cubs were 15 months old; however, the third litter was lost after two weeks and Pippa mated within one week, giving birth about three months later. Adamson noted that a cheetah in Nairobi Park had a second litter shortly after being attended by her first, from which she sneaked away to give birth. McLaughlin (1970) in Nairobi Park recorded intervals between births of 17, 18, and 19 months. Schaller (1972) reports an 18-month period between birth and conception for a Serengeti female.

Visual encounters between adult groups of both sexes or all males and the family group in Nairobi Park occurred but no further associations were observed. Schaller (1972) observed two family groups momentarily meet and then separate. Scent markings are critical for spacing of cheetah groups but they also communicate estrus condition and serve to enable males to locate females. I observed a second female in Nairobi Park that had an older litter of cubs. The female exhibited estrus when her cubs were 12–14 months old. Data on birth-to-birth and birth-to-estrus periods when cubs are not lost or removed are summarized in Table 2–3.

TABLE 2-3 BIRTH-TO-BIRTH AND BIRTH-TO-ESTRUS PERIODS WHEN LITTERS WERE NOT LOST OR REMOVED

Captive or Wild Cheetahs	Birth-to-Birth Periods (Mos.)	Birth-to-Estrus Periods (Mos.)
Captive	13	10
Captive	11	3.5
Wild (Kenya)	—	10
Wild (Kenya)	—	10
Wild (Kenya)	—	12–14
Wild (Kenya)	18	15
Wild (Kenya)	18	15
Wild (Kenya)	17	—
Wild (Kenya)	18	—
Wild (Kenya)	19	—
Wild (Tanzania)	—	18

The first recorded birth of cheetahs in captivity was in 1956 at the Philadelphia Zoo. The female gave birth to two males and one female (2:1) cub. The female killed one instantly; the two surviving cubs were removed but lived only a few days. Thirteen months later the same female gave birth to two cubs (1:1). The mother raised the cubs until they died of distemper at an age of three months.

The Krefield Zoo, Germany, had four cubs born in 1960. None of the cubs survived (Encke, 1960).

A cheetah at the Oklahoma City Zoo gave birth to two litters, three and two cubs respectively, in 1962. None survived (Thomas, 1965).

It was not until 1966 that a female in a private Roman zoo gave birth to a cub that was raised by its mother (however, with human assistance). The cub was a male. The same cheetah gave birth late in the same year to three male cubs (Florio and Spinelli, 1968).

In 1967, a cheetah at the Whipsnade Zoo gave birth to 1:2 cubs. Only one cub died but the female raised the other two (Manton, 1970). The same cheetah had a litter (1:1) in 1970, which she also raised successfully. I have been informed that one of the captive born cubs has matured and since given birth at Whipsnade. This is the first case of a second generation captive birth.

In France at the Montepellier Zoo, a litter of three cubs was born in 1968, and raised by their mother (Vallat, 1971).

At the San Diego Wild Animal Park, a cheetah from South West Africa gave birth in 1970 to three cubs, two of which were killed by a male. The surviving cub was removed and hand-raised but later died. This male cub had lived longer than any cheetah born in the U.S. (Herdman, 1973). The same female gave birth again in 1972 to three cubs, all of which survived and are being raised by their mother (Herdman, 1972).

Table 2–4 summarizes data on captive cheetah births (Thompson, in press).

In the wild, Denis (1964:40) found a litter of four cubs and refers to another of three; both litters estimated to be seven to eight weeks old. Shortridge (1934:108) tells of Wilhelm finding a litter of two cubs in South West Africa that were apparently four to six weeks old. Foster and McLaughlin (1968) report a litter of five cubs born in Nairobi Park. McLaughlin (1970) reported on six litters, from three to six cubs each, averaging 4.3. Pienaar (1963) records a litter of five cubs in Kruger Park. Adamson's (1969) cheetah had four litters under wild conditions that numbered three, four, four, and four cubs. Sex ratios in two litters were three females to one male and three males to one female. Even litters of seven to eight weeks in age may not accurately reflect birth litter size since many probably die in early life. This is indicated especially by Adamson's observations: out of eleven cubs born only three lived to adulthood and all but one of those lost died very young. Of 15 wild litters estimated less than one month old by Graham and Parker (1965:4), six had four cubs; the average size was 3.7. The largest litters ever sighted, one young and the other two older, had eight cubs. Sightings in the Cheetah Survey (Graham

TABLE 2-4   A SUMMARY OF CHEETAH BIRTHS IN CAPTIVITY
(FROM THOMPSON, IN PRESS)

Zoo	Date	No. Born	Remarks
Philadelphia, USA	24 March 1956	2, 1	
Philadelphia	25 April 1957	1, 1	
Krefeld, Germany	24 April 1960	1, 1	
Krefeld	?	?	No details
Oklahoma City, USA	7 April 1962	2, 1	
Oklahoma City	14 November 1962	2	
Arnhem, Netherlands	?	?	No details
Spinelli, Italy	13 January 1966	1	Tame pet
Spinelli	14 December 1966	3	
Whipsnade, England	15 September 1967	1, 2	
Whipsnade	22 July 1968	1, 2	
Whipsnade	6 February 1970	1, 1	
Whipsnade	7 March 1971	3	
Whipsnade	24 October 1972	?	Marvin Jones
Montpellier, France	1 December 1968	2, 1	
Montpellier	May 1970	3, 1	
San Diego, USA	22 November 1970	3	
San Diego	28 April 1972	3	
Toledo, USA	26 December 1971	1, 3	

and Parker, 1965:4) show that in older age classes litters are progressively smaller.

From these observations of young litters in the wild plus data from five litters averaging five known cubs after birth, it can be said that the average cheetah litter in the wild is at least four cubs. This assumes that some cub mortality occurs in the first six weeks. There is an obvious disparity between captive and wild litter sizes at birth. Smaller litters in captivity may be the result of physiological stress due to captive conditions or poor nutrition.

The dates of cheetah births are summarized in Table 2–5. Hamilton (1912 in Asdell, 1964:493) and Stevenson-Hamilton (1947:200) do not provide numbers of litters for their estimates of birth seasons in the latter half of the year in the Transvaal. Smithers (1966) and Ansell (1960) both record cheetah births in Zambia in November through March. All other birth dates are based on specific litters and are estimated within one to two specific months. The birth dates in East Africa and captivity indicate a primary birth season from March through June; however, Schaller's (1972) sample of 14 litters in the Serengeti indicated an even distribution of births from January to August. He observed no births between September and December. Using aging criteria of size, length of pelage, condition of teeth, and level of play behavior, Lion Country Safari received cheetahs that were apparently born in South West Africa in November, December,

TABLE 2-5 LOCATIONS AND BIRTHS IN WILD CHEETAHS

Source	Location and/or Origin	No. Litters	Wild or Captive	Birth Months
Hamilton (1912) in Asdell (1964:493)	Transvaal	—	Wild	July–December
Stevenson-Hamilton (1947:200)	Eastern Transvaal	—	Wild	June–December
Stevenson-Hamilton (1947:200)	Eastern Transvaal	—	Wild	August–December
Shortridge (1934:108)	South West Africa	1	Wild	December or January
Ansell (1960)	Northern Rhodesia	2	Wild	March or April and March
Graham and Parker (1965:8)	Nairobi National Park	2[a]	Wild	May
Graham and Parker (1965:8)	Nairobi National Park	1	Wild	August, late
Eaton	Nairobi National Park	1	Wild	May, early
Eaton	Nairobi National Park	1	Wild	April–June
Eaton	Nairobi National Park	1	Wild	November
Eaton	Masai Amboseli Game Preserve	1	Wild	April–June
Foster and McLaughlin (1968)	Nairobi National Park	1	Wild	November
Adamson (1969)	N.F.D., Kenya	2	Wild	March
		1	Wild	August
		1	Wild	July

[a] One litter of three young was estimated at about eight months old when observed in January.

and January. These same cheetahs exhibited highest mating activity in July, August, and September, implying that they would have given birth in the latter half of the year. San Diego Zoo's cheetahs, also from South West Africa, showed a similar mating season, and one of their five females gave birth in November and in April. Herdman (1972) found highest mating activity in South West African cheetahs at San Diego Wild Animal Park to be July–August and December–January. World Wildlife Safari cheetahs also from South West Africa have shown breeding in June–July and October–November.

Births appear to occur seasonally and at different times of the year in East as opposed to South Africa: 14 of the 21 more exact estimates of captive and wild litter births to cheetahs from both regions are from March through June. Peak rains for Masailand, which includes Nairobi Park and Masai Amboseli Game Reserve, are in March and April (Talbot and Talbot, 1963:16). Game is widely scattered over the plains once the rains come and large game concentrations are rare. When most litters are six to ten months old, October to February, a second but less intense and often irregular rainy season occurs. The female raising cubs goes through stages in rearing the young that vary in their demands: (1) feeding the cubs from birth to six months, by herself; (2) teaching the cubs, age 6–12 months, to hunt while still providing most of the food; and (3) hunting with the cubs, which are effective hunters, from age 12 months on. When these periods are plotted against the rainy seasons and game concentrations, which are inversely related, it is seen that the first step parallels lower game concentrations, the second phase parallels higher game concentrations, and the third stage parallels lower game concentrations again.

Factors affecting hunting success that are related to seasonal changes, other than game concentrations, are vegetation growth and color. The height of vegetation appears to change little, and may not affect cheetah activities. The color of vegetation does change distinctly. Whether or not prey species possess color vision, contrast of cheetahs to cover is probably less detectable in the dry season. In the rainy seasons, in lush green grass, cheetahs should be more visible. The second phase of cub rearing parallels not only higher game concentrations but lower visibility of cheetahs by prey. The second phase is the most difficult period for the female in rearing young for several reasons. The cubs are growing fast and demand ever-increasing diets. This food must be provided by the female until the cubs can hunt effectively by themselves. During this period the female is also teaching the young how to hunt. This requires much time and is highly unproductive; the cubs contribute very little to the family's food supply, they "scare" game away frequently, and the female's time is cut short for hunting. As the cubs approach the ability to make kills they are increasingly active in learning how to hunt, which would require increased energy expenditures. It is to be expected that natural selection would favor females that bear young at a time when they can best meet the energy requirements of the cubs. This contention is made in general by Lack (1954:64). There would be a differential reproductive success of females that give birth when the dry season does not parallel the most precarious period in rearing young. Robinette et al. (1961:210) have demonstrated that reproduction in the mountain lion (*Felis concolor*) is timed so that the small cubs are born not in the colder months but in the summer. Similar results were found by Eaton et al. (1973) in a large, captive population of mountain lion. Birth season appears to be an adaptation to prevent young from freezing while the female goes on hunts.

Seasons of birth may vary in regions with different ecological conditions. Since relatively few data on wild cheetah are available from other than East African areas, it is difficult to speculate on birth seasons elsewhere.

It is to be expected that factors such as abundance of susceptible young prey might be related to birth seasons in cheetahs. In East Africa most ungulates drop their young either throughout the year or at the onset of the rainy season. Since cheetah cubs are frequently preyed upon by other predator species and the cubs remain sedentary until they are about eight weeks old when they accompany the female, the ease of preying upon ungulates born at the onset of the rainy season could be an advantage to the female with very young cubs. Similar ecological correlation should be expected in South West African cheetahs.

MORTALITY

With the effect of hunting and economic exploitation of cheetah perhaps it is impossible to weigh the importance of various natural mortality factors on cheetah numbers. Although the natural conditions which existed before the entrance of European man into Africa are impossible to determine, present conditions in protected areas should bring basic relationships into sight.

In the field work I collected cheetah feces from at least 15 animals of four different groups, and in all 29 "scats," tape and intestinal roundworms were present. These parasites appeared plentiful but no further work was carried out with respect to internal or external parasites. No sick or dead cheetahs were acccessible for autopsy. Upon worming, Adamson's cheetah, Pippa, excreted a large tapeworm; unfortunately, it was unidentified. She did identify dog tick fever (*Babesia canis*) in young cheetah cubs. Her cheetahs were frequently covered with ticks and camel flies (hippoboscids).

The important information that has come from the intimate contacts between species of wild animals and their keepers can not be overemphasized. It is often the habit of hard-nosed experimentalists to scorn the works of naturalists or animal lovers; however, the frequent reference throughout this book to the observations of Mrs. Adamson should be testimony to the great value of her approach in uncovering hard to unravel facts. Although I could not both keep cheetahs and study them in the field in Africa, I feel that I came to know the animal much better by being able to observe them so closely at Lion Country Safari and World Wildlife Safari. It is a desirable procedure for ethologists carrying out naturalistic field studies or experimental investigations to also keep some subjects as pets just so additional insights into the species' nature will be discovered. A modern classical case is the work of Fritz Walther (1965) in which he assumed the role of mother to several young antelope. Only by acting as a member of the species could Walther unravel the processes of imprinting and how the young animal comes to know its own mother.

Disease is common in young captive cheetahs. Crandall (1964:397) points out that in many zoos felids, panleucopenia (feline distemper) is a common deadly disease in young animals including cheetahs. In fact it is panleucopenia that has largely prevented the breeding in captivity of cheetahs since they are exceptionally susceptible. Of the 11 cubs born in captivity between 1956 and 1960, eight died of panleucopenia, one was killed by the mother when she was excited, and only two lived a short while. Immunization is available but it involves a series of injections during which the cubs can contract the disease. It is not known if this disease is an important mortality factor to cheetahs in the wild, but since most mortality in the wild is explainable by factors other than disease, it is unlikely that the disease is nearly so important in natural populations. Since cheetahs are so vulnerable to panleucopenia, it is probable that they have not lived with it in the wild, or that some larger molecules (antibodies) incapable of passing through the placental barrier are transferred directly to cubs via nursing, in the mother's milk. In captivity the cubs are usually removed just after birth, thus, perhaps, prevented from acquiring immunity to panleucopenia and other communicable diseases.

Rickets is a common disease in captive cheetahs (Mercier, 1961; Young, 1967). Adamson (1969) reported rickets in free-living cubs; however, much of the cubs' food was being provided by her and since rickets is usually due to a vitamin deficiency or mineral imbalance, the occurrence of the disease in purely wild animals can not necessarily be inferred. Cheetahs, as cubs, do appear to be more susceptible to rickets than any of the other cats (Young, 1967). Gastroenteritis is brought on in cheetah cubs in several ways: changes of diet, inadequate diets, old milk, and infection from internal parasites, bacteria, and viruses (Young, 1967). Pienaar (1969) found anthrax as a cause of death, and malnourished or vitamin-deficient cubs in Kruger Park.

Post-mortem examinations on four cheetahs that died in captivity showed that two adult males both showed toxic dystrophy of the liver (Gandras and Encke, 1966). Two young females both had Laennec's cirrhosis of the liver. While in the Miami area I spoke with people who had had cheetahs that died, and the diagnosis was in each case some kind of liver ailment. This has been the most common cause of poor health in captive cheetahs. It is plausible that lack of activity could be responsible for liver disease. Few animals must rely on as specialized a liver as the cheetah, in mobilizing energy for "the fastest chase on earth."

Two cubs that died in Nairobi National Park were examined by Murray et al. (1964). They took blood smears and found severe anemia. Histological analysis turned up *Spirocera lupi* worms in the aortic media. The worms had damaged the endothelial lining of the aorta which resulted in thrombosis. In 1967 Murray found bacillary particles indicating *Eperythrozoon felis,* a cause of hemolytic anemia in house cats.

A summary of cause of death in 123 captive cheetahs is provided in Table 2-6 (derived from Van de Weaken, 1968, in Thompson, in press).

TABLE 2-6 AUTOPSY FINDINGS ON 123 CAPTIVE CHEETAHS
(DATA FROM VAN DE WEAKEN (1968),
IN THOMPSON, IN PRESS)

Post-Mortem Findings	Percentage	Average Longevity
Tuberculosis	24	2 years, 1 month
Cirrhosis of liver	11	4 years, 8 months
Other liver diseases	16	3 years, 4 months
Feline distemper	25	1 year
Pneumonia and other bronchial diseases	12	1 year, 4 months

Stevenson-Hamilton (1947:198) writes of several cases of cannibalism. In one instance a ranger saw two cheetahs fighting in a clearing of the bush and in the morning found a dead male cheetah lying where he had seen the fight. A reedbuck (*Redunca redunca*) ram lay nearby but had not been eaten, but the dead cheetah had a portion of its neck and shoulder eaten away. Stevenson-Hamilton (1947:198) records another instance in which a Major Fraser observed two large males fight until one was dead. Whether or not cannibalism exists is not nearly so important as the fact that cheetahs do exhibit actual physical aggression toward each other. Aggression is rare in that it has been recorded in the literature in only one other instance, when a male showed slight but unharmful aggression to a curious cub of a female that was apparently in estrus. I observed slight physical aggression in the wild only once, between a mother and her adult sons when they attempted to mount her. Actual aggression is sometimes a mortality factor in some species, and often it plays a function in population regulation. Hundreds of fights that I observed between wild cheetahs at Lion Country Safari resulted in not one serious injury.

The threat of aggression has replaced physical aggression for the most part. Aggression leading to physical combat resulting in death is surely not a means of population control. The threat of aggression plays a different role from combative, injurious aggression; it does not eliminate individuals but rather acts as a spacing mechanism between groups and maintains social order within groups. Aggressive behavior is described in detail below.

The effect of injuries on an animal so completely dependent on its highly specialized anatomy for survival are bound to be important. Graham and Parker (1965:18) give data on seven cheetahs with limps and another cheetah with an injured back. Adamson's (1969) cheetahs, both adult and cubs, suffered many leg injuries, some of which were analyzed as fractures, to the long bones. Starvation as a result of injury is to be expected and would have to be considered indirectly as accidental death. Several cheetahs at Lion Country Safari had old leg and foot injuries, and some became injured in captivity. Steel traps used to capture cheetahs alive probably account for the damaged feet and legs in Lion Country Safari cheetahs.

Actual starvation from lack of food directly and not as an indirect effect of disease or injury would be almost impossible to determine unless carcasses were closely examined. Three adult cheetahs have been found dead, cause unknown, and one adult with three cubs was recorded as very thin and weak (Graham and Parker, 1965:18). D. O. Thompson (pers. comm.) came upon a starving cheetah in Kenya. In descriptions of this type it is impossible to tell what caused weakness or death.

Predation on cheetahs by other predators appears to be important as a mortality factor. Graham and Parker (1965:18) recorded the following: three cases of lions feeding on cheetahs and one of leopard; two cases in the Serengeti of hyena chasing very young cheetahs with no intervention by the adults; and two animals with parts of their tails missing. Lions have attempted to catch young cheetahs in Nairobi Park. Schaller (1972) recorded a cheetah killed by a leopard, and an emaciated female killed by lions.

Data on six litters, five in Nairobi Park and one in Masai Amboseli Game Reserve, indicate that predation is an important mortality factor of cheetah cubs, or indirectly, when parent cheetahs are killed. In Masai Amboseli Game Reserve, where hyena are very common, two cubs of a litter of five were killed by hyena according to one of the native rangers. In Nairobi Park, two cubs of a litter of four were lost during one night. A litter of five newly born cubs and an adult female suddenly disappeared in Nairobi Park according to park records. A litter of five cubs lost one cub according to park records and another litter of six cubs was lost entirely.

Also, I observed a female with three cubs in which the female did not return from a hunt. The possibility of poaching or accidental death is highly unlikely in the central part of the park where she left her cubs and was last seen. Hunts away from the cubs seldom last more than a couple of hours. The female did not return that day and the cubs began running wildly; they did not eat or hunt. It is probable that they died of starvation if not from predators. It is possible that the female fell prey to the park's central pride of lions which had their main territory near where the female separated from the cubs.

The litter in Nairobi Park that lost two cubs (Fig. 1–7) during the evening of December 15, 1966, were quite healthy on that day and I left them when they were bedded down at 7:00 P.M. Previously, they could always be found in the morning where they had been left the prior evening, but early on the morning of December 16, I discovered them gone from the bed site and spotted them later about half a mile away. There were only two of the four cubs with the female. The three of them behaved quite unusually. They were extremely wary and were not nearly as approachable as before. The mother walked with her ears back and was more observant of the immediate terrain than usual. She and the two cubs darted and ran at the slightest sounds or upon my approach to normally unheeded distances. The only conclusion that I can come to is that the cubs probably were killed by other predators. Since Nairobi Park is almost never frequented by hyena or hunting dog and since it is believed that leopards are solitary and hunt alone and could not probably kill two half-grown cubs at the same time, lions seem the most likely cause of death of the two cubs. Also, since lions hunt in groups, it would be easier for them to kill more than one cub once the group was startled. There are no data from the wild which indicate that other cheetahs also prey on cubs; however, it should be expected, and has been observed in semicaptive cheetahs (Herdman, 1973).

Adamson (1969) is convinced that a hyena killed Pippa's four newly born cheetah cubs. Predation accounts for at least half the losses to her cheetah's four litters. These data of 36 cubs include only two direct observations of actual predation. Still, I think that predation is the obvious explanation for most cub losses. All of the cubs were less than ten months old. This agrees with Graham (1966:53), who points out that between one and ten months, litters decrease by about one-half in number of cubs, from 3.7 to 2.0 cubs per litter. McLaughlin (1970) reported 43% mortality in Nairobi Park litters, thus corroborating my earlier study there, and both our studies agree with Pienaar (1969), who recorded about 50% mortality in Kruger Park.

The hypothesis that predation on cheetah cubs is the most important natural limiting factor on cheetahs is supported further by the inverse relationships between cheetah group size (and abundance) in an area with the abundance of other predators. More field work is required to test this hypothesis.

⑧ *Ecology*

POPULATION PARAMETERS

Robinette et al. (1961) used weight and length to describe a growth curve for young cougar. Bobcat are aged with the cementum layers in the cainine teeth. The only method that has been used to age cheetah is a system of five general age classes based on how large cubs are relative to an adult (Graham and Parker, 1965; Graham, 1966).

Some characters are distinctive to certain age classes. Shortridge (1934:108) related the sharpness of claws to age, and Stevenson-Hamilton (1947) noted the age of first climbing. Age criteria that depend on capturing animals are undesirable when visual measures are possible from a distance.

Two-week-old cubs are covered on their upper parts with blue-gray fine hair, while the sides, tail, belly, and legs are covered with dark, solid spots. At three months cubs begin losing the long gray hair and dark spots become apparent all over the body (Fig. 3–1). Morris (1965:323) says that the mane, which Stevenson-Hamilton (1947:199) described as being lost in the third month, disappears after the tenth week at the same time that the cubs lose the ability to retract their claws. The cubs are blind at birth and the spots are present under the gray fur (Shortridge, 1934:108; Sterndale, 1884:203). These observations were confirmed by Adamson (pers. comm.,

1969) and her observations on maturation are summarized in Table 3–1.

It is appropriate here to theorize why I believe the stripe, or tear line as it is sometimes referred to, has evolved in the cheetah face. It could be important to identify members of the species and I have experimentally verified this using mounted specimens of cheetah and leopard at Lion Country Safari. In addition, it seems reasonable to suppose that the stripe breaks up the continuity and shape of the head (Fig. 3–2). It detracts especially from the large eyes. A human observer or a potential prey animal has its perceptual expectancy disrupted by the stripes. The cheetah is a diurnal predator and when it hunts it never takes its eyes off of the prey, often holding the head up in clear view above the vegetation while stalking. The stripes are really only obvious when the observer looks straight on at the cheetah's face and this is exactly the view that prey get when being stalked. Also plausible is the function of reducing glare.

TABLE 3-1   MATURATIONAL DATA DERIVED FROM ADAMSON (1969)

Age	Morphological or Behavioral Changes
5 days	Eyes shut, orient to sounds and respond by "spitting"
9 days	Cubs standing, greet mother
11 days	Eyes open
12 days	No teeth, stalking
14 days	Climb well, cling to roof of cage (Stevenson-Hamilton, 1947)
21 days	Walk steadily, "chirp" call attracts mother
28 days	Teeth irrupting
190 days	Permanent molars
240 days	Canines, last of first set of teeth, lost
245 days	Lower incisors irrupt

The stages following the loss of the gray outer fur and dark undersides are more or less continuous through the adult stage. The only differences apparent to an observer are size. Elephants (Laws, 1966:31) are aged by relative size comparisons. In the Serengeti, Schaller (1972) classed cubs by age as follows: 0–3 months—black cubs; 3–6 months—small cubs, one-half size of mother; 6–12 months—medium size, two-thirds size of mother; and older than 12 months—large cubs, distinguished from mother by more slender build and small ruff on the nape. To develop a suitable system of aging animals in the field, it is necessary to have known aged animals that can be weighed, measured, and photographed weekly during development. Sets of diagrams or illustrations could then be used in the field to age animals without having to capture them. Herdman (1972) should be able to offer such a system based on the development of captive cubs at San Diego Wild Animal Park.

The use of "cap-chur" equipment to immobilize ("dart") animals for

Figure 3–1   Cheetah cubs have a silver gray mantle until about three months old. (Photo: N. Myers.)

Figure 3–2   Hunting in tall grass, Nairobi Park. (Photo: R. L. Eaton.)

weight and measures of length could be employed to provide a series of measurements so that estimates of age would improve in accuracy. However, drugging inevitably leads to some losses and usually the knowledge gained counterbalances such losses. But in an endangered species the use of any technique that entails only occasional losses can hardly be justified. There are additional considerations with the use of drugs for capture. Unless an entire family is captured at one time, which is in itself very difficult, a cub, once recovered from the effects of the drugs, may get left behind in which case it would die. In my field study it would have been very useful to capture cheetahs with drugs and place radio transmitters on them so they could be located readily. Only one group can be kept track of at one time and each time I wanted to observe a different group it had to be searched out. Because of the hazards of immobilizing techniques, the idea was abandoned. However, York (1973) of Lion Country Safari has carefully established dosages of several drugs that can be safely used to immobilize cheetahs, and Herdman (1973) had similar success. Neither lost any cheetahs.

There are very little data on sex and age ratios. Graham (1966:51) gives sexes and groupings for 47 adult cheetahs, unaccompanied by young. The ratio of males to females for these groups is almost exactly 5:1 (males:females). In addition the Cheetah Survey (Graham and Parker, 1965:3) provides the sexes of 17 adult cheetahs that were shot, poached, or killed. There were 12 males and 5 females, bringing the ratio from the combined data to 4:1 in favor of males. The ratio appears unusually high. Schaller (1972) said the sex ratio in the Serengeti was 1:2 while Eloff reports (pers. comm.) a 3:1 in Kruger Park. We have no idea why such diverging sex ratios obtain in different areas, if in fact they do.

Graham and Parker (1965:2) compiled 1225 sightings of 2785 individual cheetahs. Of 2095 adult animals 1794 or 85% were adults, 301 or 15% were adults accompanied by litters. Of the 253 litters seen with adults, 160 or 63% were seen with one adult, 62 or 26% of the litters were seen with more than one adult, and, 31 or 12% were not seen with adults.

I think that most of the 31 litters not seen with adults must have had an adult female mother that was probably not recorded due to being present but not observed, and more likely was off hunting. Although Graham and Parker (1965:3) do not have data on the sex of the 160 single adults seen with litters, I am sure that almost all of these adults were females. Of the 62 litters seen with one or more adults (141), 62 adults can be assumed to be female mothers and 79 to be adults in groups comprising roughly 64 males and 15 females in which the males of the groups were pursuing mothers in "heat."

In the Serengeti, Schaller (1972) observed 244 individuals not accompanied by cubs; 52% were solitary, 31% were in groups of two, 14% in groups of three, and 3% in groups of four. As in Nairobi National Park, Schaller never observed a female with young accompanied by other adults or a second litter. Serengeti females are unsociable except when mating or when they have cubs, and males may form social bands with other males (Schaller, 1972), just as I observed in Nairobi Park.

In Nairobi Park I found seven males and four females among resident adults and an adult male and one female among nonresident adults. In the Amboseli area I observed three males and one female among adults. For both areas the sex ratio for adults was about 2:1.

Sex ratio data in the Cheetah Survey (Graham and Parker, 1965) are probably biased by observational factors related to movements and activities cf cheetahs, which are quite different for adult groups compared with family groups. In some areas such as Nairobi National Park, observers see adult groups more readily than litters, while in the Serengeti more frequent sightings of litters means fewer sightings of adult males and the total sex ratio is biased in the female direction. Why group compositions vary between areas is unknown unless higher early litter mortality discriminates against the latter formation of male groups.

Data on sex ratios in young are relatively rare. Graham and Parker (1965) record the sex of one litter. Very young cubs are not individually marked and it is hard to know just which cub one is observing. For this reason it is difficult to sex an entire litter, that is unless the observer can see the genitalia of all cubs at the same time!

In one litter of four cubs, I saw two males and one female but was never able to sex all four at the same time. In another litter of four cubs there were two males and two females. Another litter had two males and three females. For 13 wild cubs, 12 were sexed and the ratio was 1:1. In the litter recorded in the Cheetah Survey (Graham and Parker, 1965:9) there were originally five cubs. After one cub disappeared, there were two males and two females. These data all point to an even sex ratio for wild litters, but it is important to know sex ratios at birth and all these cubs were several months old.

Schaller (1972) sexed five 0–3 month old litters from which some cubs had already disappeared. He found 4 males and 7 females. McLaughlin (1970) in Nairobi Park found 9 of 11 cubs to be males. In older cubs, Schaller reports 10 males and 18 females, and says, "an equal sex ratio at birth seems probable."

All the cheetahs I sexed were at least five months old. In many species it has been found that there is differential infant mortality of the sexes. This possibility cannot be accounted for in the cheetah.

Longevity is an important factor when considering population dynamics and productivity. More important than longevity is period of reproductive activity. Nonreproductive members of the population can be important in other ways than actual reproduction. They can be valuable for survival of other individuals, for example if they are leaders of groups. In carnivores such as the mountain lion (Young and Goldman, 1946:87; Hornocker, 1970), learning from conspecifics, the mother in felids, is important and the value of older, more experienced individuals cannot be overestimated.

When advocating the existence of altruism or self-sacrifice in a species the problem is to determine the selective advantage to the altruistic individual's genes. In cheetahs, adult females do stay with young a short while after they have learned to hunt effectively. Continued teaching of the cubs should not counterbalance the advantage to the female in rearing still more young. The 14–16 months that a female spends with a litter indicates that learning is an important aspect of female-young relationships.

Adaptive modification of behavior (learning) gives selective advantage only to those males that can remain alive to pass on their genes and to females to remain alive, reproductive, and functioning as a parent. Burton (1962:187) gives up to 16 years for life span. Flower (1931) gives three ages for cheetahs in captivity: 13 years, 6 months; 14 years; and 15 years, 7 months in captivity. He also says that cheetahs seldom live more than six years in captivity, but Crandall (1964:398) says it is even less. Graham and Parker (1965:17) give seven years for a captive cheetah. In 1970 I discovered a pet cheetah in southern California that was 19 years old. In the wild, mortality appears much greater in cubs than in adults. Their attempts to defend kills against hyena, leopard, lion, and wild dog are usually futile. The cheetah's great fear of lions implies their vulnerability to other predators. Indeed, even adult cheetahs are killed by other predators, especially lions. Average life span of adults in the wild may be relatively short. Selection forces appear to have increased litter size and frequency of birth compared with other larger cats, implying that length of reproductive life may be relatively short, or mortality of young is high, which is fairly obvious.

Robinette et al. (1961:212) and Hornocker (1970) point out that in mountain lions, as in cheetahs, the female stays with her cubs for about two years. Mountain lions have two or three cubs per litter and give birth at about two year intervals in absence of litter mortality. The cougar has a smaller litter size and reproduces less frequently than the cheetah. Its lower reproductive potential correlates with less mortality from other predators, and apparently cougars are seldom inflicted with disease (Hornocker, 1970). Hornocker (1970) has found that the training period of the cubs is prolonged and rigorous, more so than earlier believed.

Cheetahs average at least four cubs per litter and often come into estrus while the litter is still being raised. Females with litters mate as soon as 10–12 months after parturition in the absence of litter mortality. Allowing for a three months gestation period, births are sometimes 13–15 months apart, a higher frequency than any other big cat. Since mating by females with cubs often occurs more than three months prior to the time when the first litter strikes out on its own, there may be delayed implantation of the embryo which is known to occur in cougars (Robinette et al., 1961:216) and house cats (Asdell, 1964:168).

The only wild individuals on which I have dates for determining longevity is a group of males in Nairobi Park. Park records, photographs, and Graham and Parker's data all lead to the conclusion that a group of four males were mature in July, 1964. In fact, they must have been more than 14 months old since they were exceptionally large at that time. A photograph of a nearly mature litter (Fig. 3–3) with the mother shows how the young adults are not as heavy in build though they are 14–16 months old.

Putting the four brothers' age at a minimum of 16 months in July, 1964, their age (only two of them were present in February, 1967) at the termination of the field study was 47 months. They appeared to be in peak physical condition, were the largest cheetahs I ever saw, and were the most effective hunters. Their teeth appeared perfect and they dispatched and ate prey easily. It appears that four years is prime age for males.

Pippa, Joy Adamson's cheetah, was four and one-half years old in July, 1968. She was apparently quite healthy and certainly was reproductively active. Pippa conceived the first time at about 22 months. Age of sexual maturity in females is given by Varaday (1966) who also kept a pet cheetah that he let run free on his farm in South Africa. His female came into her first estrus at two years. In the Serengeti, one female conceived at 21 months, and another exhibited behavioral estrus at 22 months (Schaller, 1972). Cheetah females apparently mature sexually at an earlier age than mountain lions (Robinette et al. 1961) or lions (Asdell, 1964) in which 30–36 months is usual; however, the earliest record of age at first birth is 24 months, for a lioness at Lion Country Safari (Eaton, 1972).

The age composition of a population is crucial if one is to understand population trends. Natality and mortality have considerable influence on the age composition and vice-versa as Alexander (1958:136) sets forth.

To really understand a population's trends and to be able to predict its future one must have data over several years. With the cheetah it is desirable to evaluate the annual cyclic environmental changes and how they effect productivity. The age makeup of a population at any point in time should be present in the data of 2785 cheetah observed in East Africa. The age composition of these cheetah was 2095 adults and 690 immatures or 75% adults and 25% immatures, an adult to young ratio of 3:1. This ratio appears entirely too large.

Cheetahs are more difficult to observe the younger they are. As they

Figure 3–3 A family group of a female and four nearly mature young (14–16 months) shows that the mother, second from the right, is larger and heavier. One male cub took over leadership of the entire family but was not allowed to mate with his mother when she came into heat. (Photo: R. L. Eaton.)

mature they are much more active and are larger, both of which should increase observability. Beyond about six months of age observer bias should decrease since cubs then begin hunting with the adult at least some of the time, and are more active and less secretive.

Graham and Parker (1965:5) present data on the age groups of the immatures observed. Litter size increased with progressive age until the four to seven months category. It is hardly imaginable that numbers of litters should increase with age. They should stay the same or decrease with age. Again, more data on the fate of litters from birth are necessary.

The only way that a 3:1 age ratio can be productive is if there is hardly any mortality between birth and reproductive age. That this is not the case is obvious. Level of mortality in the reproductive or postreproductive part of the life span is unknown. Mortality may be higher for females as indicated by the exaggerated sex ratio in adults in some areas.

The postreproductive age mortality is probably quite high for the few cheetah that may live this long. There appears to be selection favoring only the reproductively active individuals in the population; however, there are no aging techniques for adults, and there is no information that relates mortality to adult age.

Since many adult groups are well recognized and known to have remained together in nearly every case, it is believed that mortality to members of all-adult groups is relatively low. Adult groups are almost always males, and females should suffer higher mortality due to rearing young. The nature of social organization in cheetahs appears to account for the high sex ratio. Where cub mortality is low, for example where other predators are less numerous, groups should be larger and males might be expected to predominate in the local sex ratio which would be even more exaggerated since observers see adult groups more readily than single females or females with cubs. In those areas where adult groups are not common, sex ratios should be lower and more accurate since solitary individuals should be encountered equally regardless of sex. Data on sex ratios in different regions are sparse. In Kruger Park where lions and hyenas are not abundant, the sex ratio is largely (3:1) in favor of males. Nairobi Park, low in hyena, has a high sex ratio. In the Serengeti, where other larger predators are most dense, there appears to be a sex ratio in favor of females. The missing link in these speculations is whether or not males separate and live singly as adults in some areas, for example where availability or size of prey would favor a modified social life. Ecological conditions could easily account for such social artifacts; however, we simply lack data from several long-term studies carried out in different regions.

PREDATOR-PREY ECOLOGY

Equatorial Africa has the richest mammalian fauna in the world. "Nowhere else in the world is there to be found so many species of wild ungulates, many of which have extremely large populations" (Bourliere, 1963). Because of this great array of both individuals and species of wildlife, this area has great aesthetic value. In order to preserve the wildlife of Africa in the face of rapid population growth many biologists have advocated the use of surpluses of natural animal populations for food rather than attempting to replace them with domestic livestock (Bourliere, 1963; Darling, 1960). The wise management of the wild animal resources can be carried out effectively only if the ecology of these species is thoroughly understood.

Ecologists are studying these natural communities, especially the ungulate herbivores since they make up the great potential for human food. Until recently less attention has been paid to the larger carnivores. Vesey-FitzGerald (1960) suggests that in the Rukwa Valley predators (lion, leopard, and hunting dog) are not important in limiting prey but rather the alternating seasons of flood and drought and its effects on the herbage. On the other hand, the Talbots (1963) argue that on the Serengeti-Mara Plains of East Africa the lion is limiting the numbers of wildebeests by taking up to a third of the population per year. Bourliere (1963) presents data from the Ruindi-Rutshuru Plains and Nairobi and Kruger National Parks to support his hypothesis that carnivores (lion, leopard, cheetah, and wild hunting dogs) play an important role in controlling the size of herbivore populations, at least for several of the prey species.

The diversity of opinion on the role of predators in controlling prey populations is not new. Errington (1946) for example has argued from years of work on muskrat (*Ondatra zibethicus*) ecology that losses due to predation are incidental and that habitat conditions are what limits the herbivore. Laboratory experimentation and theoretical speculations, on the other hand, have suggested that many herbivores are predator-limited, not food-limited. At least for Africa this question is of vital importance for the continued survival of the large predators in any kind of management scheme.

Investigations by Kühme (1965), Guggisberg (1963), Wright (1960), and Schenkel (1966) have added information on the African lions ecology and mating behavior. The first full-scale field studies have just been conducted by Schaller (1972) and Eloff (1973) on the lion. Kruuk (1972) has conducted a long-term study of the hyena (*Crocutus* c.). Estes and Goddard (1967) studied the hunting dog (*Lycaon pictus*), and Wyman (1967) the jackal (*Canis mesomelas*). Observations on the leopard are relatively rare (Bourliere, 1963b; Schaller, 1972), due to the fact that they live mostly in riverine bush where observation is difficult. Because the lion has attracted the attention of sportsmen and biologists, much more is known of its general ecology (Fig. 3–4). Schaller's long-term study (1972) adds greatly to an overall understanding of the lion and its role in the community.

Previous conclusions on cheetah biology should be evaluated with skepticism. Most observers have marveled at the cheetah's speed and relative ease with which it should procure a meal; but purely on the basis of deductive inference from evolutionary theory, can it therefore be surmised that the cheetah has adapted to small, swift antelope but that the

Figure 3–4 The lion has been the subject of several studies in East Africa. (Photo: N. Myers.)

antelope are helpless? If this were true then we would expect the cheetah to overeat its prey, which it does not. The prey, as Klopfer (1964) states, usually adapts as a function of the predator's capabilities, and one goal of the field biologist is to unravel the intricate behavioral adaptations that have evolved between hunter and hunted in their never-ending race of adaptation.

A number of excellent recent studies (Bourliere, 1963; Foster and Kearney, 1967; Graham, 1966; Hornocker, 1969; Kruuk and Turner, 1967; Schaller, 1972; Wright, 1957; Joslin, 1973; Eloff, 1973; Muckenhirm and Eisenberg, 1973) have contributed to our knowledge of the predator-prey ecology and behavior of the big cats.

It was pointed out that to describe a predator's energy budget, it is not sufficient to give the percentage of occurrence of each prey species in the predator's diet. Wright (1957, and pers. comm.), for example, lost much valuable information in his pioneering study of African predators in that he located carcasses usually long after the animal had been killed and largely consumed by predators and scavengers. Foster and Kearney (1967:118) point out a similar limitation in their study: "The smaller species are probably always under-represented due to the rapidity with which they are eaten." Young prey with soft, edible bones are either more quickly or more completely eaten, and both cases lead to biases in data which are gathered by examination of prey remains (Fig. 3–5).

In many studies on carnivores in African parks, much of the data are collected by indirect and nonrandom means, such as using vultures which locate kills in more open areas, and on reports of visitors and park personnel who largely frequent the more accessible areas. Round-the-clock observation of a predator provides important information by which data gathered in other ways can be more objectively evaluated to determine the factors related to successful predation by cheetah and to examine regional differences and similarities in food habits, prey selection, and hunting techniques. This same principle emerges from Schaller's (1972) study of cheetah predation in the Serengeti, where the ages of prey varied significantly when Schaller (or others) actually observed killing as opposed to examining prey discovered after it was killed.

FOOD HABITS

A total of 27 species have been recorded as cheetah kills in East Africa (Graham, 1966). Pienaar (1969) listed 24 species for Kruger National Park, and 9 species are recorded as prey in the Serengeti (Schaller, 1972). The variety of prey ranges from hares and newly born warthogs to adult wildebeests and zebra—a weight range of less than 5 to 600 pounds (weights after Bourliere, 1963). Impala, Grant's gazelle, and Thomson's gazelle, which as adults average 120–160, 130–155, and 40–50 pounds respectively, comprise about two-thirds of all recorded kills in East Africa (Graham, 1966). In the Serengeti, a lot of cheetah kills were Thomson's gazelles, by far the most abundant prey species. (Schaller, 1972).

TABLE 3–2 WEIGHTS OF KILLS OF NAIROBI NATIONAL PARK
CHEETAH GROUPS

Group	N	Range (Lbs.)	Mean Weight (Lbs.)
1	17	10–150	75
2	7	30–150	124.2
3	3	10–600	185.0
4	3	10–130	67.0
			$m = 112.8$

The average field-estimated weight of all cheetah kills observed was 113 pounds. The average for each group varied from 67 pounds for group 4 to 185 pounds for group 3 (Table 3–2).

In Nairobi National Park, impala (*Aepyceros melampus*), Grant's gazelle

Figure 3–5 A family group feeding on Thomson's gazelle in Amboseli, Kenya. (Photo: H. Patel.)

(*Gazella granti*), kongoni (*Alcelaphus buselaphus*), and waterbuck (*Kobus ellipsiprymnus*) occur most frequently in the cheetah's diet. A preference quotient, $\dfrac{relative\ frequency\ in\ diet}{relative\ frequency\ of\ abundance}$ shows a value of 1.0 or higher for impala, Grant's gazelle, and waterbuck but less than 1.0 for kongoni (Table 3–3). Reedbuck (*Redunca redunca*) show the high value of 18 but they are relatively rare and unimportant overall as cheetah prey. It should be noted that McLaughlin (1970) found Thomson's gazelle to be more important prey in Nairobi Park than I did, but this was not unexpected since his study was longer than mine. Further, after my study, water was made available year-round in the park, thus keeping "Thommies" there. Unlike Grant's gazelles, Thommies require water daily. Moreover, the entire critical result of my analysis of predation (Eaton, 1970) was that intergroup variation was high, and can be expected to vary over time with new specializations or preferences of succeeding generations. Students of carnivores should thus be cautioned to expect striking differences in individuals and groups in the same area, and also in different populations.

Observations by ten observers (pers. comm.) in Nairobi Park during my study total 23 kills (Table 3–4). Of the 14 aged kills, 13 were adults,

TABLE 3-3 INDEX OF PREFERENCE OF CHEETAH PREY SPECIES
IN NAIROBI NATIONAL PARK[a]

Species	Relative Frequency of Abundance	Relative Frequency of Diet	Diet/Abundance Index
Kongoni	.26	.10	.38
Impala	.16	.433	2.7
Grant's Gazelle	.13	.166	1.2
Thomson's Gazelle	.092	.033	.35
Waterbuck	.024	.133	5.5
Wildebeest	.067	.00	—
Reedbuck[b]	.0018	.033	18.0
Warthog	.041	.10	2.4
Zebra	.126	.00	—
Ostrich	.025	.00	—

Relative frequency of abundance computed from Foster and Kearney, 1967.
[b] Species not listed in Foster and Kearney but Nairobi National Park censuses in October and November, 1966, average = 7.

compared with my observations of 12 adults and 18 juveniles. Ten of the 12 adults were females. When lumped, the two sets of data show a preponderance of adults and a near-even sex ratio.

Of 16 species in the park known to be cheetah prey, ten were hunted and seven were killed. Park records, visitor's observations, and photographs show that of the three species not killed in my observations, zebra and wildebeest have been taken in the park while steinbuck (*Raphicerus campestris*) kills were not recorded; however, they were hunted.

Group 1 hunted seven species and killed all but one—steinbuck. Group 1's hunt/kill ratio was 5:1. About one-half of its kills were impala, 3:1. Grant's gazelle, second most important in diet was second in hunt/kill, 5:1. Thomson's gazelle and kongoni were hunted frequently but show a high hunt/kill ratio (that is, low success).

The adult female's eight impala kills (Table 3–5) include four adults; the only male was weak and apparently quite old. Observations by others give adult females and juveniles for six of seven kills.

Group 2 hunted five and killed two species. Their overall hunt/kill is 3.5:1.0. They were especially effective with waterbuck, hunt/kill = 2.0:1.0. A preference quotient shows waterbuck highly vulnerable to this group. All the waterbucks were subadults and the impalas were adult females.

Group 3 hunted four species, killing kongoni and warthog. The group originally consisted of four males, thought to be brothers, and are known to have killed adult zebra, wildebeeste, waterbuck, ostrich, and Grant's gazelles. The Nairobi Park records and two of my observations show kongoni as most important in this group's diet. They show a hunt/kill of 2:1 for all prey. All kills in park records are listed as adults, sex unknown. The warthog was newly born and killed by one of the group when the two separated temporarily. Both kongoni kills from which I collected skulls and additional kills aged by M. Gosling (pers. comm.) were subadult males about 14 months old.

Group 4 hunted five species, killing three. Their hunt/kill was 4:1. Their three kills included a newly born warthog, an adult female Grant's gazelle and a juvenile male impala.

HUNTING BEHAVIOR

There is much disagreement on the hunting behavior of the cheetah. Kruuk and Turner (1967:21) conclude that cheetah are "almost entirely solitary" hunters in the Serengeti. On the other hand Bourliere (1963)

TABLE 3-4

A. COMPILED KILL DATA FROM TEN OBSERVERS IN NAIROBI NATIONAL PARK DURING THE PERIOD OF THE STUDY

	Adult			Juvenile				
	Male	Female	?	Male	Female	?	?	Total
Impala	1	2	—	—	—	—	3	6
Grant's Gazelle	2	1	—	—	—	—	1	4
Thomson's Gazelle	3	—	—	—	—	—	1	4
Kongoni	—	—	—	—	—	—	2	2
Waterbuck	—	—	—	—	—	—	1	1
Warthog	—	—	—	—	—	1	—	1
Wildebeest	—	—	1	—	—	—	—	1
Zebra	—	—	1	—	—	—	—	1
Reedbuck	—	1	—	—	—	—	1	2
Ostrich	—	1	—	—	—	—	—	1
Total	6	5	2	—	—	1	9	23

B. MY OBSERVATIONS OVER THE SAME PERIOD

	Adult			Juvenile				
	Male	Female	?	Male	Female	?	?	Total
Impala	1	7	—	2	3	—	—	13
Grant's Gazelle	—	2	—	2	—	1	—	5
Thomson's Gazelle	—	1	—	—	—	—	—	1
Kongoni	—	—	—	2	—	1	—	3
Waterbuck	—	—	—	2	1	1	—	4
Warthog	—	—	—	—	—	3	—	3
Wildebeest	—	—	—	—	—	—	—	—
Zebra	—	—	—	—	—	—	—	—
Reedbuck	1	—	—	—	—	—	—	1
Ostrich	—	—	—	—	—	—	—	—
Total	2	10	—	8	4	6	—	30

TABLE 3-5 THE IMPALA KILLS OF THE SINGLE ADULT OF GROUP 1

Impala	Sex	Adult	Juvenile	Estimated Weight	Condition
1	m	x		120	poor
2	m		x	20	good
3	f		x	40	good
4	f	x		100	good
5	f	x		100	good
6	f		x	40	good
7	?		x	40	good
8	f	x		100	good
Total	5 f 2 m 1 ?	4	4	$m = 70$ pounds	

states, "Only those predators like . . . the cheetah . . . that hunt their prey in organized groups may succeed in overcoming animals much larger than themselves. . . ."

Schaller (1968:98–99) reports hunts by a single hunting female with cubs only, and makes no mention of adult group hunting. Estes (1967a:46) says that cheetahs are "open pursuit" and "solitary" hunters as opposed to "stalk-pounce" and "gregarious" hunters. Walther (1969) observed 88 hunts by single cheetah in the Serengeti. De Vore and Washburn (1963:364) observed five cheetahs kill an impala in Nairobi Park. Graham and Parker (1965:19) say, "In the adult segment of the population unaccompanied by immatures, single animals are the most common grouping everywhere except Nairobi Park, where twos are the most common . . . except the Serengeti Park where singles are most frequent." Pienaar (1968) reports that cheetahs are seen in groups (at least two) or families in Kruger Park more frequently than singly.

Conclusions about the structure and size of hunting cheetah groups are misleading due to regional differences in ecology and consequently litter and adult group sizes. The above divergent views reflect the differences that do exist from area to area.

The differences in prey size and species preyed upon in any area is in part a function of the size of the hunting group. Kruuk and Turner's (1967) data on 23 kills, when fitted to prey weights, show an average prey size of 83.5 pounds, about 30 pounds less than the average of 30 kills in Nairobi National Park. Schaller's (1968:95–96) kill data show an average prey size even smaller since 121 of the 136 kills were Thomson's gazelles in his data.

The fact that Thomson's gazelle is the most abundant cheetah prey in the Serengeti may make it uneconomical for anything but single cheetah to hunt this area's most predictable prey item. Cheetah prey most on Thomson's gazelle in the Serengeti (Graham, 1966; Kruuk and Turner, 1967;

and H. F. Lamprey, pers. comm.). Selection may disfavor group hunting there; however, it is reasonable to suppose that selection favors group hunting of larger species, and that other ecological factors, such as predation on litters, limit group size and therefore prey size.

I observed hunting by 15 cheetahs comprising the four groups in Nairobi Park. They offered a variety of sex and age compositions for comparison (Table 3–6). Because of the cohesiveness of adult or family groups each group can be considered functionally as a separate, distinct hunting unit. Nearly all hunting was done by the entire family or adult group, only rarely by single individuals. At no time did one group cooperatively hunt with another, though cooperation within groups did occur.

Descriptions of hunting vary widely. Graham and Parker (1965:13) analyzed 40 eyewitness accounts of cheetahs making kills; all except two involved either a direct approach or stalking of the prey followed by a rush. The gap between predator and prey was usually 70–100 yards.

In the Serengeti, Walther (1970) relates that cheetahs approach to hunting distance, 150–250 meters, lie down, sit, or stand, then attack. Stalks were rarely seen as opposed to open approaches. Kruuk and Turner (1967:13) say, ". . . the stalking part of the hunt seemed virtually absent in this species. It walked over the open plains towards a potential prey . . . and caught the prey after a chase of several hundred meters." They often observed cheetah cubs stalking in play. Schaller's (1968:9) observations of 40 hunts by an adult female show that stalking was an important element of this (Serengeti) cheetah's hunting behavior.

Pienaar (1968) relates that cheetahs do stalk in Kruger Park. There, impala, which prefer wooded savanna, are the principal prey, and stalking is to be expected.

The hunting technique of open pursuit is probably more common in the Serengeti than in Nairobi Park. Cheetahs hunting in habitats that offer cover, such as most of Nairobi Park, stalk the prey, but in open short-grass plains, for example part of Nairobi Park and much of the Serengeti area,

TABLE 3–6 HUNT-TO-KILL RATIOS FOR NAIROBI NATIONAL PARK CHEETAH GROUPS

Group	Hunts	Kills	Hunt/Kill
1	115	17	6.1/1.0
2	24	7	3.5/1.0
3	6	3	2.0/1.0
4	12	3	4.0/1.0
Totals 4	157	30	$m = 5.2/1.0$ (for all observations)[a]

[a] Unweighted mean hunt/kill for all groups = 3.8/1.0.

open pursuit is employed. In Masai Amboseli Game Reserve's open, flat plains, where ground cover is scarce, a cheetah with cubs stalked by crawling on the ground before attacking. Since cheetah cubs stalk in the Serengeti but adults seldom do, stalking must be a portion of the innate predatory sequence but later "drops out" with hunting experience.

In areas conducive for only open pursuit hunting, where prey are also usually aware of the predator, the cheetah's role is more one of a natural culler of less fit individuals from prey populations. In such areas, cheetahs appear to prey more selectively by making a greater number of hunts per unit time and kill, and thereby sample prey herds for less fit animals more effectively. Schaller's (1972) study of cheetah in the Serengeti indicates that old animals are killed slightly more often than expected. His data agree with Walther's (1970) in that a disproportionately greater number of adult females are taken.

A hunt can arbitrarily be divided into a stalk and an attack. This division is artificial in that a hunt may consist of a stalk or an attack but not both. For instance, prey have stumbled onto resting or hiding cheetah and an overt attack occurred without a prior stalk. Also, cheetahs, in spite of a careful stalk, were often discovered by the intended prey and an attack was not made. Here a hunt is described as either a stalk or an attack or both, a kill being a successful hunt.

Factors related to hunting success are many—prey species (sex, age, condition, etc.), herd size, cover type, prey responses before attack, prey responses during attack, number of hunting cheetahs, distance of chee-tah's attack, cheetah-prey distance when prey ran, and cheetah-prey distance when cheetah attacked. A hunt-to-kill ratio is applied to each of these factors in order to evaluate their importance.

For the four groups in Nairobi Park, the cumulative data show a hunt-to-kill ratio of 5.2:1.0 (Table 3–6). The individual groups show differences, which on the basis of hunts per kills indicate an order from most to least successful: 3, 2, 4, and 1.

SIZE OF PREY HERDS, HABITAT AND OTHER FACTORS

There are no data available as to frequency of herd size for the species in Nairobi Park, only monthly censuses (Foster and Kearney, 1967). When hunted herds are arbitrarily divided into sizes (Table 3–7, it is seen that of 157 hunts, 136 were of herds numbering 30 or less. One to five is the most commonly hunted herd size, with 1–5, 6–10, 11–20, 21–30, having an average hunt/kill ratio of 5.1:1, about equal to the ratio for all herd sizes, 5.2:1. The single hunting female of group 1 hunted herds of 1–30 70% of the time. She hunted Grant's gazelle, Thomson's gazelle, impala, and

TABLE 3-7 GROUP HUNT/KILL RATIOS RELATED TO PREY HERD SIZES

Herd Size	Group 1	2	3	4	Total
1–5	7:1(28:4)	4:1(16:4)	4:1(4:1)	2.5:1(5:2)	4.8:1(53:11)
6–10	5.1:1(26:5)	2:1(4:2)	—	2:0(2:0)	4.6:1(32:7)
11–20	8.7:1(26:3)	2:1(2:1)	—	3:1(3:1)	6.1:1(31:5)
21–30	5:1(15:3)	2:0(2:0)	1:1(1:1)	2:0(2:0)	5:1(20:4)
31–40	4:0(4:0)	—	—	—	4:0(4:0)
41–50	6:1(6:1)	—	1:1(1:1)	—	3.5:1(7:2)
51–100	7:0(7:0)	—	—	—	7:0(7:0)
101+	1:1(1:1)	—	—	—	1:1(1:1)
Total	115:17	24:7	6:3	12:3	5.2:1(157:30)

kongoni 60% of the time. These species appeared in herds of 1–30 animals frequently.

Seventy-five percent of Group 2's hunts and 57% of their kills were of herds numbering 1–5. Waterbuck, this group's principal prey, were seen most frequently in small bands. Group 3 hunted 1–5 animals four times; its kongoni kills were from herds of 21–30 and 41–50. Several kongoni kills (M. Gosling, pers. comm.) were from hunts of large herds. Group 4 hunted herds from 1 to 30; one of its three kills was a warthog, a species found in family groups of 1–5.

Acacia-grassland savanna is about equal in total area with open grassland plains in Nairobi Park. All groups' home ranges overlapped. Of four cover types (Table 3–8) there were, for all groups, 83 hunts and 13 kills in Acacia-grassland savanna, 52 hunts and 12 kills in open grassland, 12 hunts and 4 kills in heavy bush, and 10 hunts with one kill in marshy habitat.

Group 1, the female with small cubs, hunted mostly in Acacia-grassland savanna where it made 9 of its 17 kills. This group was the only one to hunt in either heavy bush or marsh. The mother's hunts were particularly successful just inside heavy bush areas adjacent to savanna or plains (Fig.

TABLE 3-8 HUNT/KILL RATIOS IN THE HABITAT TYPES OF
NAIROBI NATIONAL PARK

Group	Acacia- Grassland Savanna	Open Grassland Plains	Heavy Bush	Marsh	Total
1	7.7:1(70:9)	7.7:1(23:3)	3:1(12:4)	10:1(10:1)	115:17
2	—	3.4:1(24:7)	—	—	24:7
3	2:1(4:2)	2:1(2:1)	—	—	6:3
4	4.5:1(9:2)	3:1(3:1)	—	—	12:3
Total 4	6.4:1(83.13)	4.3:1(52:12)	3:1(12:4)	10:1(10:1)	157:30

Figure 3–6 One female that had four cubs (group 1) was highly successful at hunting impala which frequent the heavier bush. Most hunts by cheetahs are in more open areas, but this individual hunted in habitat that is typical of the leopard's. (Photo: R. L. Eaton.)

3–6). Her kills were impala, which frequent the woody, more dense areas more than other important prey. An observation by R. Casebeer (pers. comm.) and mine of the adult female of group 1 killing a reedbuck constitute the only two kills of the rarest, in occurrence, cheetah prey species in the park. The preference quotient for reedbuck is 18 for all cheetahs' kills but even higher for group 1.

Both reedbuck kills and seven more hunts were around the edges of the same small marsh. Marshes constitute less than 1% of the park's total area. No other cheetahs were observed hunting in marshes.

Group 2 with five adults often moved into savanna but did their hunting in the open plains along the Athi River bush area where their principal prey—waterbuck—were concentrated, though not abundant.

The two males of Group 3, formerly of the four male group, hunted in both *Acacia* savanna and in the open plains where kongoni were found. Park records showed this group in only these two cover types. The original group and the two remaining individuals hunted and killed the largest species known to be cheetah prey.

Group 4 with three adults hunted in the same habitat as group 3; however, they never hunted or killed the four larger species that group 3 did. Impala and Grant's gazelle were the largest species they hunted.

For all observed kills, if hunting success is related to the prey's responses before attacked then the hunt/kill is 12.7:1 when prey are aware as opposed to 2.0:1.0 for unaware prey (Table 3–9).

TABLE 3–9 HUNT/KILL RATIOS RELATED TO PREY RESPONSE BEFORE ATTACKED

Group	Aware	Unaware
1	85:1 ($N = 85$)	30:16 ($N = 30$)
2	4.2:1 ($N = 17$)	2.3:1 ($N = 7$)
3	2.5:1 ($N = 5$)	1:1 ($N = 1$)
4	5:1 ($N = 5$)	3.5:1 ($N = 7$)
Total	14.9:1 ($N = 107$)	2:1 ($N = 45$)

The success of the group 1 cheetah depended almost entirely on the prey being unaware prior to attack. The prey were much less vulnerable when they were aware. This cheetah typically underwent extensive stalks sometimes involving several hours in which only a few yards were traversed. Where open spaces separated the cheetah from a herd the cheetah often hid in cover. If the herd grazed closer the cheetah waited until they were close enough to attack (Fig. 3–7). In cases where the prey saw the cheetah, snorting alerted all prey species in the vicinity which often led to "mobbing" of the cheetah. Prey animals often searched out and followed the cheetah as it moved off, snorting as they went and alerting other potential prey along the way. This procedure often continued until the cheetah had moved completely out of range of any prey.

Group 2 showed a higher hunting success when prey were unaware but were more successful with aware prey than was group 1. The cover type of open plains by necessity made stalking less important than overt attacks. This group hunted in the same way as described for cheetahs in the open

Figure 3–7 Starting out on a hunt employing sparse ground cover in open plains. (Photo: H. Patel.)

plains of the Serengeti (Kruuk and Turner, 1967) where prey are usually aware of cheetah prior to an attack.

Hunts by groups 3 and 4 were not frequently observed; however, the two males of group 3 depended on kongoni being aware. It is the antipredator attack by yearling males that enabled them to kill kongoni so readily.

Using only those hunts including an attack, hunting success is related to the prey's response during the attack (Table 3–10).

The prey's responses are divided into five classes: (1) prey (2 or more) ran together at the same time; (2) not together; (3) not at the same time; (4) not together and not at the same time; and (5) antipredator attack by the prey. The hunt/kill is 4.3:1.0 or less for all categories of prey response except for response 1 which is 9.5:1.0.

Group 1's hunter, the mother, had a low hunt/kill ratio (higher success) when prey did not run together or at the same time. More total kills were made when they responded to the attack by not running together simultaneously. When this cheetah attacked juvenile kongonis, yearling males responded by charging, and the cheetah turned and fled.

Group 2 had no success when the prey responded to attack by running as a herd at the same time. Whenever one or more of a herd ran before the

TABLE 3-10 HUNTING SUCCESS RELATED TO PREY RESPONSES
DURING ATTACK
HUNTS WITH NO ATTACK ARE EXCLUDED

Preys' (Two or More) Response	Group				Total
	1	2	3	4	
1 Ran together at same time	9:1 (N = 53)	8:0 (N = 8)	—	6:1 (N = 6)	9.5:1 (N = 67)
2 Not together	7:1(21:3)	1:1 (N = 2)	—	3:1 (N = 3)	4.3:1 (N = 26)
3 Not at same time	6:1 (N = 17)	1:1 (N = 3)	—	2:1 (N = 2)	3:1 (N = 22)
4 Both 2 and 3	—	—	1:1 (N = 1)	—	1:1 (N = 1)
5 Antipredator attack	4:0 (N = 4)	2:0 (N = 2)	1:1 (N = 2)	—	3.5:1 (N = 7)

rest of the herd, or when the herd separated, then a kill was made. Antipredator attacks by kongoni deterred this group's attacks.

The only kill by group 3 of other than kongoni was observed when one of the two males killed a newly born warthog. In this case the cheetah was 30 yards from an adult warthog and two young before the warthogs were alerted. The two young ran one way, the adult ran the other. The cheetah pursued the young and in the meantime the adult turned around and pursued the cheetah. When one young warthog was caught the adult circled twice around the cheetah within five feet before running off after its surviving young.

Group 4 showed a lower hunt/kill when the herd escape response was not a cohesive one. Whenever a warthog with young was aware of the cheetah before they were close, or if the warthogs had a good head start, the adult female turned to face the cheetah with her young standing directly under her stomach. Individuals of the cheetah group surrounded the warthogs, charging in turn at them but were not successful in separating adult from young unless the warthogs turned and fled.

Hunting success was related to cheetah-prey distances when prey ran as opposed to cheetah-prey distance when cheetah ran (Table 3–11). These data exclude hunts consisting of a stalk only. In unsuccessful hunts the distance between predator and prey when the prey ran averaged 157.2 yards, the distance when the cheetah ran averaged 217 yards. In successful hunts the average distance for all observations when the prey ran was 50.4 yards and for cheetah it was 58 yards.

Group 1 killed when it was on the average 56 yards from the prey when it attacked and then it ran 20 yards before the prey ran.

In unsuccessful hunts the female also attacked before the prey fled but not always.

Group 2 usually did not attack until the prey had already run. In many cases the cheetahs simply walked toward a herd until an animal ran and they pursued it. These five cheetah were on the average 81 yards from the prey when their pursuit ended in a kill.

On unsuccessful hunts they often began running toward prey at distances up to 400 yards. In these hunts the prey were alerted before the cheetahs were close enough to pose a real threat and they escaped easily. Although four of the five cheetah were nearly mature they were less experienced than their mother. The hunts involving attacks of great length were always led by the younger cheetah.

The males of group 3 had very small distances between them and the prey when they attacked. This is partly due to the fact that in two of the three kills they simply loped toward kongoni when, at about 60 yards, a kongoni attacked the cheetah. When the kongoni had come about 25 yards closer, the two males attacked and killed it.

TABLE 3–11 HUNTING SUCCESS RELATED TO CHEETAH-PREY DISTANCES[a]

	Group 1		Group 2		Group 3		Group 4	
	Unsucc. N = 66	Succ. 17	Unsucc. 5	Succ. 7	Unsucc. —	Succ. 3	Unsucc. 8	Succ. 3
Distances (yards) when prey ran	80.4	36.2	234	65	—	50	120	65
Distances when cheetah ran	96	56	338	81	—	37[b]	100	80
Averages	88.2	46.1	286	73	—	43.5	110	72.5

[a] Includes only those hunts where distances could be measured or estimated with relative accuracy.
[b] Two of the three kills involved antipredator attack by kongoni.

Group 4 attacked the prey on the average just before it ran. For the hunts that were successful the group averaged a distance of 58 yards between it and the prey when the cheetah attacked.

The importance of continuous field observations in arriving at an accurate assessment of predatory behavior and ecology is obvious. The accumulation of kill data by chance observations, as for example from park personnel or visitors, cannot be considered random. Nairobi Park's visitors' records indicate an entirely different species, age, and sex composition of cheetah prey from mine. By following a cheetah, a family, or an adult group it is possible to establish the similarities and differences between hunting units.

Pienaar's (1968) data on cheetah predation in Kruger Park is based on carcass location and not direct observation; he speculates that many smaller species of birds and mammals and the young of smaller antelope species probably are quite important as prey. In Nairobi Park no hunts or kills of birds other than ostrich have been observed or recorded. The point is that in any one area, behavioral data should supplement carcass data as a means of properly assessing a predator's ecological role in the community.

PREY SELECTION

It was shown that the largest prey were killed by groups but there is not a constant relationship between group size and size of prey, for example some groups killed the same size prey as single hunting cheetah. In the same local area, groups presumably equal in killing effectiveness show quite different kill data.

Graham and Parker (1965) conclude that "there is no tendency to select juvenile animals as 79 percent of all kills are of adult animals." Their data show a two to one sex ratio of adult males to adult females; however, 92 of 130 adult kills were not sexed. Estes (1967:201–202) states that cheetah select adult gazelles when hunting. Wright (1960:8) shows that of those kills aged and sexed, all were males and five of seven were adult. Kruuk and Turner's (1967:14–15) data give adult Thomson's gazelles as the most important diet item—52%. Of seven Thomson's gazelles sexed, six were females. F. Walther (pers. comm., 1969) in the Serengeti observed cheetah kill Thomson's gazelles. His observations show a remarkable nonrandom selection of females from predominantly male adult herds and subadult males from bachelor herds.

Pienaar (1969) shows for Kruger Park a nonrandom selection of juveniles, and among adults, a 2:1 ratio of females to males. Schaller (1968:96) shows that a cheetah pursued a small fawn whenever it was available, and had 100% hunting success with that age group.

In order to establish the importance of selection of prey by predator, it must be demonstrated that the kills comprise other than a random sample of the prey populations. Walther's and Schaller's data specifically support the view that cheetahs discriminate age and sex differences in prey and that (either innately or learned or both) cheetah hunt and kill the more vulnerable prey. Walther's data on flight distances in the different sex and age groups correspond directly with cheetah prey selection. It is to be expected that selection would favor greater flight distances to predators in the prey classes most vulnerable to predation.

It is interesting that in many prey species the territorial male is under the influence of conflicting pressures of natural selection. On the one hand is the selection for differential reproductive success, higher as a result of an individual's territoriality, while on the other hand is the greater vulnerability to dangers, such as predators, against which the herd is supposedly the best defense. If territorial Thomson's gazelles are most susceptible to predation, kill data and flight distances should indicate it.

Flight distances are shortest for territorial males and Walther (1969) noted that they were preyed upon proportionately less than bachelor herd males or females. Thomson's gazelles in the Serengeti defend territories for the most part in flat, open plains that offer good vision, while bachelor males are found where open plains and bush meet, the area of greatest ease for predators to make kills. It is to be expected that predation of "thommies" in areas of homogeneous habitats would probably show that flight distances of territorial males is closer to that of bachelor males and females and that kills are more evenly distributed between these classes.

In the group of two males, learning, probably quite by accident, determined selection of kongoni as their principal prey. The group of five preyed heavily on waterbuck which abound only in the locality in which the four cubs were reared by the female. The killing of waterbuck by the mother may have been a necessity, but the selection of waterbuck by the grown cubs is now traditional, undoubtedly the result of learning and possibly a kind of imprinting.

Specialization on different prey by cheetah in the same area certainly occurs, and regional differences, though often reflecting prey abundance, may be partially the result of specialization.

The impala is the most abundant prey species in Kruger Park but ranks only fifth in terms of preference; two species—reedbuck and waterbuck—that occur also in Nairobi National Park are preferred by cheetahs in both areas.

In Kruger Park (Pienaar, 1969, and pers. comm.) reedbuck have the highest preference of all cheetah prey. In fact, the cheetah is the most important predator of reedbuck there, responsible for 21.76% of all predator mortality. What is peculiar is that in Kafue National Park, Zambia, reedbuck are more abundant than in Kruger and yet are not an important cheetah prey according to Mitchell et all. (1965).

The "habit image" offered to explain the preference by lions for wildebeeste in Nairobi Park (Foster and Kearney, 1967) indicated a common specialization for prey by different prides. This implies less inter-group variation in prey selection by lions than exists for cheetah in Nairobi Park.

Newly born warthogs are common prey for cheetah, but adult warthogs are avoided altogether. The same is reported for Kruger Park (Pienaar, 1968). That cheetah of different groups show this common avoidance implies an ability to recognize particular qualities of particular species. It is conceivable that cubs learn to hunt only what their mother hunts and that once learned, only particular prey stimuli release the predatory sequence of behavior. How discrimination between young and adult warthogs is made is not known unless it is by trial and error in which cases a cub would likely be injured or killed. Lions (*Panthera leo*) are killed by warthogs (Watt, 1968:135) and tigers (*Panthera tigris*) by wild boar (*Sus scrofa*) (Schaller, 1967). Several studies (Estes, 1967; Wright, 1960; Kruuk and Turner, 1967) disagree on which classes of prey are differentially selected by cheetah. Walther's (1969) data and Schaller's (1968:97) continuous observations of one cheetah's hunts show a selection of females over males in adult herds and of juveniles over adults. Recognition and selection of juveniles from adults could be based on size; however, female adults in typical cheetah species are barely smaller than males. In impala, recognition could be by presence or absence of horns but both sexes of the gazelle species are horned. This explanation is confounded by flight distances of prey. Females with greater flight distances may, by running first from a herd, cause visual fixation by the cheetah on them, and release the cheetah's attack.

Driver and Humphries (1967) pointed out experimentally that in order for a predator to respond effectively to fleeing prey, response time must be cut down by fixating on one of many prey stimuli. In the Serengeti, differential flight distance may lead to differential predation but in Nairobi Park cheetah often attack *before* prey take flight and still differential selection of prey is apparent. Kruuk and Turner (1967) observed a cheetah that was not able to kill an adult Grant's gazelle. Such experiences could enable cheetah to learn to discriminate males from females; if so, one-trial learning would be adaptive since such encounters could be injurious.

In the case of group 3's predation on subadult male kongoni, the apparent selection of male prey is only an artifact of the kongoni's antipredator behavior.

PREFERENCE AND VULNERABILITY OF PREY

Wright (1960:10) says, "Seven predators preyed upon impala, although it is comparatively few in numbers." Wright (1960:11) assigns relative vulnerability to prey species according to the number of predators that kill them. This scale takes no account of prey species' abundance, or availability to the predator. Schaller (pers. comm. in Foster and Kearney, 1967:118) notes that lions choose larger over smaller prey when both appear equally available. Foster and Kearney (1967:118) propose that lions form an "habitual prey image" of abundant species and this results in differential predation of these prey species even when their populations have declined to levels lower than other prey apparently of the same "preyability." Guggisberg (1961) applies the term "habit killers" to lions to describe their ability to specialize on certain prey species. Bourlière (1963) compares the relative frequency of the different ungulate species as prey of the lion with the abundance of these prey in three parks. Bourliere does not give any kind of value that demonstrates the presence or absence of preference for certain prey by lions. It is obvious that abundance alone is not the only factor determining prey selection. Bourliere postulates palatability as possibly influencing prey selection.

I have applied the preference quotient to cheetah kill data from the Serengeti (Table 3–12), using one million as the approximate Serengeti ungulate population from various estimates. Kruuk and Turner's 23 recorded cheetah kills show that the most important prey, Thomson's gazelle, are not killed any more than they occur. Kruuk and Turner's data show that kongoni are the most vulnerable prey, while wildebeeste (juveniles), the second most important prey in diet, are taken less than they abound.

Schaller (1968:95–96) shows quite different species selection in the Serengeti. Schaller's data on 136 kills (40 hunts were observed) show Thomson's gazelles occurring as prey 88% of the time, far greater than they

TABLE 3–12   THE PREFERENCE-VULNERABILITY QUOTIENT APPLIED
TO PREY CENSUSES OF THE SERENGETI AND KRUUK
AND TURNER'S (1967) CHEETAH KILL DATA

Prey Species	Relative Frequency of Abundance	Relative Frequency of Diet	Preference-Vulnerability Index
Wildebeest	.33	.26	0.78
Kongoni	.0013	.087	66.0
Zebra	.16	.043	.27
Thomson's gazelle	.50	.56	1.12
Hare[a]	—	.087	—

[a] No estimates of abundance.

occur. Schaller pointed out that actual availability of Thomson's gazelles is greater in the cheetah's preferred hunting habitat, since during the dry season they are highly concentrated in the plains and practically the only prey species available.

In Kruger Park impala made up 47 of 65 (73%) cheetah kills while impala comprise 83% of the ungulate population there (Bourliere, 1964). It appears that impala are not especially vulnerable or preferred there.

If a prey species occurs in the diet at a higher level than its relative abundance, it could be either more vulnerable or preferred or both. Wright's scale of relative vulnerability of prey is based on occurrence in the diet of several predators. Vulnerability scales should be related to abundance of prey and more specifically to relative availability. The prey's visitation to the predator's area should give an even more accurate picture of prey vulnerability.

The application of the index of preference shows that relative availability or abundance is not the only factor determining prey selection. Here it is assumed that in general preference for a prey represents the prey's vulnerability; however, biochemical deterrents affecting palatability certainly are possible. That vulnerability may not be a direct measure of preference is shown by group 1 in which the female hunted several species equally but killed chiefly only one. Although this cheetah's kills give the impression that it specializes on and therefore "prefers" impala, its hunts show that impala are vulnerable but not necessarily preferred. This hypothesis is not borne out in predation of reedbuck by cheetah in which reedbuck are rare but are highly vulnerable; or by wildebeest in Nairobi Park that have shown a continued high vulnerability to lions in spite of a vastly decreasing population. Since the reedbuck habitat in Nairobi Park consists of small isolated marshes, heavy predation pressure is to be expected. The marshes are scarce enough to allow ease of predation but limit population growth.

The data from four descriptions by Kruuk and Turner (1967) show that cheetah attacks averaged 183.3 yards and that the cheetah-prey distance when cheetah attacked averaged 95 yards. Cheetah began their attack before the prey ran and overcame the prey after it fled for 88.3 yards. All these kills were in the open plains of the Serengeti, none of which involved a stalk. In all cases the prey were aware of the cheetah prior to the attack.

Walther (1969), working on gazelles, observed 88 hunts by single cheetah, of which seven were successful, a hunt/kill ratio of 12.5:1. In the successful hunts cheetah attacked from 150–200 yards. The average flight distance from cheetah was 200–300 yards, rarely less than 100 or more than 600 yards, varying with the prey species and age or sex classes. Contray to Kruuk and Turner's observations the cheetah often did not attack until the prey had taken flight.

Schaller (1968:98–99) describes hunting in one cheetah, the behavior of which corresponds closely to the female with cubs in Nairobi Park (group 1). He does not quantify the cheetah's behavior, so it is difficult to make comparisons. Schaller describes a "typical hunt"; however, in Nairobi Park hunting was typical only within a group. It would be helpful to have accurate descriptions of several cheetahs, single and in groups, in the Serengeti, so the factors related to regional differences—cover types, prey species, etc.—could be assessed. Nairobi Park data imply that hunting is in large part a product of a particular cheetah's or group's hunting experience.

The lower hunt/kill ratio for Nairobi Park cheetahs as compared to Serengeti cheetah may indicate that the best cheetah habitat is other than strictly open plains; however, kills are made no more frequently in Nairobi Park. The open plains of the Serengeti demand an open pursuit hunt which is by its nature less economical in number of hunts but more economical in that it is less time consuming than the stalk-attack hunt common in Nairobi Park.

Group comparisons in Nairobi Park show that the single hunter requires more hunts per kill than a group but groups vary. The most efficient group had two cheetahs and this group also showed the highest prey specialization, which for them was more efficient in terms of reward for energy expended.

Hunting success was higher in herds of 30 or less. Larger herds presumably offer a greater predator alarm system; however, the threshold for "alert" may be lower in smaller herds which may result in each individual being more alert than if in a larger herd. Although difficult to quantify, the individuals in very small herds appeared to spend more time being alert and watching for predators than did animals in larger herds. The "fear" of predators often resulted in flight in small impala herds without the alarm calls and intense watching associated with the predator alarm system of the larger herds. Although it has not been studied, flight distances may be found to vary as a function of herd size.

The predator-reaction system in the prey is probably a compromise of two selection factors. On the one hand there is selective advantage to individuals that are wary and alert for predators, while on the other hand, any herbivore must spend a large part of its time and energy eating. The final product of selection forces is a behavioral repertoire that includes, for most individuals, the optimal balance of energy expenditure for predator alertness and eating. Individuals that deviate from this optimal and delicate energy budget are probably selected against by either being nutritionally less fit or the obvious disadvantage of being killed by predators. The regularity of five to seven minutes for "staring contests" between slightly alerted prey in smaller herds and the cheetah reflects this principle, that is, this time span, afforded for a low level of arousal, is optimal for determining potential danger without taking too much time away from eating which is also of great survival value to herbivores.

Condition may have been an important factor in selection of prey by cheetah but in only one case was poor condition of prey apparent. Schaller (1968) noted that none of the kills he saw appeared to be of prey in poor condition. This study should have employed techniques to determine prey condition, for example bone marrow analysis.

Hunting success was higher when prey were not aware before attacked. The hunt/kill ratio when prey were aware prior to attack in Nairobi Park is almost identical to that for the Serengeti, where prey are almost always aware before attacked.

The hunt/kill ratios for prey response during attack indicates that flight of the prey as a tightly knit herd reduces predation.

The failure of an individual of a herd to respond in the same way as the others increases its chances of being singled out and killed. The abnormal flight responses of a particular animal may indicate a higher vulnerability and this may explain the release of the cheetah's attack when one or more animals take flight before the rest of the herd.

It appears that cheetah seldom make kills when they attack at greater than 200 yards and hunting success increases the shorter the distance is between cheetah and prey. Perhaps the cheetah depends on its ability to assess the weakening of prey while chasing it, for in many cases the cheetah would stop pursuit even though it appeared to be closing the gap between it and the prey.

DETAILED DESCRIPTIONS OF SPECIFIC HUNTS

As was stated above, it is not possible to describe a typical hunt for the cheetah since so many variables affect any particular hunt. But in order to provide specific accounts in detail I have selected a day's hunts for each of three groups in Nairobi Park (Tables 3–13, 3–14, and 3–15). Some hunts are graphically depicted in Figs. 3–8–3–11.

ENERGY BUDGETS

The number of possible hunts involving a chase is limited by the time spent in finding, stalking, and pursuing prey. The limitations set by the output of time and energy in hunting must be balanced by the input into the system which is the energy derived from eating captured prey. Data on the actual energy expended in hunting could only be measured by knowing oxygen consumption during all activities, calories and materials used to maintain bodily functions, the loss of energy in excretions, etc. These data cannot be gathered under field conditions.

The only measure of expenditure of energy in hunting was breathing rates. Breathing rates were recorded on several occasions. The data presented (Table 3–16) were recorded in Nairobi Park at an altitude of nearly a mile, all near mid-day with partial cloud cover (field estimates 15–20%) and similar temperatures, close to 80°F on each day cited.

The few data indicate that the cheetah's adaptations for speed include a capacity for large changes in respiratory rate. Rates ranged from 16 for one adult male lying in shade to 156 for a second adult male following a chase and prolonged kill by strangulation. The latter male's respiratory rate may have been unusually high due to the inhibition of respiratory recovery involved in the maintenance of the strangle hold on the prey. Another

TABLE 3-13 HUNTING DAY OF GROUP 1, DECEMBER 17, 1966

Species Hunted	Sex	Age	Cond.	Cover	Herd Makeup	Response Before Attack	Response During Attack	Distance Stalked	Distance Chased	Kill
Grant's Gazelle	m	ad.	good	grass, open	30 Grant's & Thommies	Aware, 2 m Grant's ran from herd, cheetah pursued	2 Grant's ran, kept 200 yards from cheetah	0	300 yards	No
Impala	m f	ad.	good	Acacia, high grass	2 f & 1 m impala	Ran just before attack	Ran together, directly away from cheetah	25 yards	25 yards	No
Grant's Gazelle	f	ad.	good	Acacia, high grass	4 f Grant's	Ran when downwind without seeing cheetah	No attack	30 yards	0	No
Reedbuck	—	ad.	good	heavy marsh	1	Ran from marsh, not seen by cheetah	No attack	40 yards	0	No
Kongoni	m f	2 ad. 1 juv.	good	grass, open, cheetah in gulley	3	Unaware, walking single file right angle to cheetah	m kongoni attacked cheetah, then f, juv. ran, f pursued cheetah	30	50	No
Warthog	f	1 ad. 2 juv.	good	Acacia-savanna	3	Unaware	Cheetah separated f from juvs., 1 juv. into hole, other escaped	30	150	No
Thomson's Gazelle	—	ad.	good	Acacia-savanna	20	Aware, ran	1 lagged behind herd, was chased	20	100	No
Grant's Gazelle	f	ad.	good	Acacia-savanna	4	Aware, ran	No attack	20	0	No
Impala	m f	ad. juv.	good	shrub, heavy	30 f 10 juv. 1 m	Staring contests	Herd split up, ran in different directions	60	50	Yes, juv. m

TABLE 3-14 HUNTING DAY OF GROUP 2, JANUARY 22, 1967

Species Hunted	Sex	Age	Cond.	Herd Makeup	Response Before Attack	Response During Attack	Dist. Stalk	Dist. Chase	Kill	Comments
Impala	f	ad.	good	1	Aware, standing watching cheetahs	Ran	200	300	0	Leader cub led chase, followed by mother only
Kongoni	m f	ad.	good	30	3 m ads. closest to cheetahs watching & alarm calls, rest of herd—f & juv. ran off 100 yards watching cheetahs, ad. f cheetah stalked, cubs not move, 3 m kongonis ran	No attack, f called cubs to her	150	0	0	F cheetah continued stalk but all prey alert and watching her
Waterbuck	1 m 2 f	ad. ad.	good	3	Aware, watching cheetahs	Ran cohesively	200	0	0	Leader cub kept breaking from stalk and running at prey
Impala	4 f 1 m 2 —	5 ad. 2 juv.	good	7	Unaware	Ran cohesively	0	300	0	As running toward impalas cheetahs alerted waterbuck chased earlier which alerted impalas
Impala	m	ad.	good	20 kongoni 1 zebra 1 giraffe 1 waterbuck 1 impala	Aware, 1 m kongoni approaches the cheetahs while stalking, impala broke and ran first then herd ran in different direction	Ran, not with herd	200	300	0	Lead cub only chased impala (See Fig. 3-11.)

TABLE 3-14 (continued)

Species Hunted	Sex	Age	Cond.	Herd Makeup	Response Before Attack	Response During Attack	Dist. Stalk	Dist. Chase	Kill	Comments
Impala	f	ad.	good	1	Unaware of cheetah but staring contest with stalking lion	No attack	100	0	0	Lead cub saw lioness when 200 yards away from impala & lion. Stopped hunt. Kongoni alarm to cheetah alerted impala which ran, lion not follow
Waterbuck	f	2 ad. 1 juv.	good	3	Unaware	1 ad. into bush, others into open	250	140	x	Lead m cub chased ad. & juv., they saw other cheetahs & split, lead cub killed juv.

TABLE 3-15 HUNTING DAY OF GROUP 3, DECEMBER 28, 1966 (ONE OF TWO MALES HUNTING)

Species Hunted	Sex	Age	Cond.	Cover	Herd Makeup	Response Before Attack	Response During Attack	Dist. Stalk	Dist. Chase	Kill	Comments
Warthog	f	1 ad. 2 juv.	good	Acacia, grassland dense	3	Unaware, feeding	Juvs. ran one way, f ran other	10	110	x	See Fig. 3–8.

HUNTING DAY OF GROUP 3, JANUARY 17, 1967 (BOTH MALES HUNTING)

| Kongoni | m f | ads. & juvs. | good | Acacia, grassland open | 30 | Unaware | Subadult m attacked cheetahs | 70 | 50 | x | See Fig. 3–10. |

HUNTING DAY OF FEMALE AND TWO CUBS, MASAI AMBOSELI GAME RESERVE, JANUARY 4, 1967

| Thommie | m | ads. | good | grassland flat, open | 15 Thommies | Unaware | All but 2 ran one direction, cheetah chased these 2 | 250 | 140 | x | Cheetah stalked over barren ground |

adult, a female, exhibited 136 and 140 respirations per minute, 2 and 6 minutes, respectively, after an extensive chase. It appears that lying down is less efficient for recovery following a chase, presumably as a result of a decrease in expansion of the rib cage in the prone position.

TABLE 3-16

Date, Time	Activities	Respiration/Minute
11/18/66, 10:35 A.M.	Adult female chases prey	
11:00	Female sitting on haunches, proceeded by slow walking	60
2:18 P.M.	Same female and its six month old cubs chase prey	
2:20	All cheetahs lying down in partial shade:	
	female	136
	cubs	176
2:24	Female	140
	Cubs	168
2:27	Cheetahs walk slowly to and lie down in full shade	
2:38	Female	60
	Cubs	
11/20/66, 10:30 A.M.	Three adult cheetahs walking slowly	
11:00	Cheetahs walk to shade, lie down	
11:30	One male, lying down	16
12/28/66, 11:30 A.M.	Adult male chases, catches, and carries live juvenile warthog (*Phacochoerus aethopleus* Pallas) to shade, lies down holding warthog in mouth	
11:45	Warthog dies from strangle hold, cheetah remains lying down	156
11:48	Cheetah sitting on haunches	112
11:49	Cheetah lying down	126
11:55	Cheetah, still lying, licks blood from carcass	120
12:00	Cheetah feeds on rear quarters	115
12:05 P.M.	Still feeding, intermittently sits up, looks around	

That recovery ratio limits the number of full-intensity chases relative to time was indicated by an observation of an adult cheetah which had just chased prey unsuccessfully and came upon a steinbuck (*Raphicerus campestris* Thunberg) that ran from the cheetah at a distance of a few feet, but was pursued only momentarily. The cheetah's respiratory rate appeared very high just before encountering the steinbuck and probably precluded a second chase immediately following the first. It is also typical for cheetahs to seek and lie down in shade following an unsuccessful chase for one-half hour before resuming hunting. It appears reasonable to assume that the movement to shade facilitates respiratory recovery; however, this same movement with prey would be adaptive in preventing localization by other predators or scavengers.

BIOMASS TRANSFER

The possibility of using the wild ungulates of Africa as a protein source for the African makes it necessary to evaluate the effects of the predators on the wild populations. Maximum figures for the effects of the cheetah on its prey are used in calculating how much live weight is taken by them. Nairobi National Park has the highest density of cheetah known.

Using 25 adult cheetah as the park's maximum population in an area of

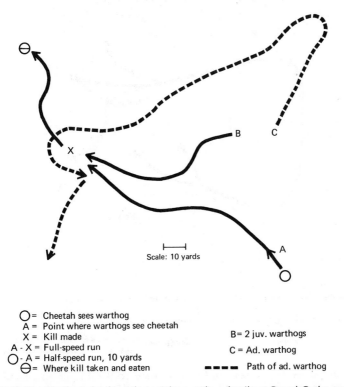

O = Cheetah sees warthog
A = Point where warthogs see cheetah
X = Kill made
A - X = Full-speed run
O - A = Half-speed run, 10 yards
⊖ = Where kill taken and eaten

B = 2 juv. warthogs
C = Ad. warthog
■ ■ ■ ■ Path of ad. warthog

Scale: 10 yards

Figure 3–8 The single male cheetah saw the warthog family at B and C, the two piglets grazing away from their mother. The cheetah started running slowly towards the piglets at location B but was quickly seen by them. They ran away from their mother who then took flight in a different direction. The cheetah intercepted the young and caught one of them before the mother warthog circled back to defend her young. As the cheetah held its prey the mother charged nearby and then ran off after the other piglet. If the three warthogs had escaped together in the same direction, there probably would have been no kill.

44 square miles gives a density of about .6 cheetah per square mile. Again, for maximum predation, we shall assign body weights of 120 pounds to each of the 25 cheetah. The park's game herds must support 3000 pounds of cheetah or 72 cheetah-pounds/square mile. (See Fig. 3–12.) Each day the cheetah eats a maximum of 1.0 pounds/10 pounds of body weight. This means that the maximum consumption is 12 pounds/day/cheetah or 400 pounds/day for all the 25 cheetah, which is 146,000 pounds per year. The average total prey weight per square mile in Nairobi Park is 71,294 pounds for the year. For each pound of meat consumed by cheetah there is a maximum of another one-half pound wasted in skin bones and

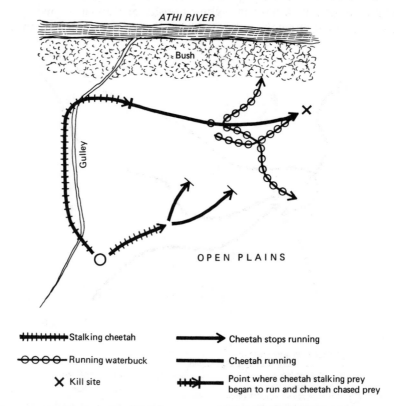

++++++++ Stalking cheetah	⟶ Cheetah stops running
⊖⊖⊖⊖ Running waterbuck	▬▬▬ Cheetah running
✕ Kill site	++▷▬ Point where cheetah stalking prey began to run and cheetah chased prey

Figure 3–9 A female cheetah and her four nearly adult cubs sighted a band of three waterbuck. The mother separated from her litter and made an indirect stalk utilizing a gulley and its cover. The younger cheetahs stalked slowly towards the waterbuck. As the adult cheetah stalked away from the gulley she was in less cover and was seen by the waterbuck. The escape pattern of the three prey was discoordinated. One adult ran towards the heavy cover by the river. The two juvenile waterbuck ran in the same direction momentarily but then saw the younger cheetahs, now attacking. One of the waterbuck cut back towards the river and the adult cheetah and was killed.

uneaten entrails. The 146,000 pounds actually consumed by cheetahs converts to 219,000 pounds of total prey killed.

The maximum predation for each square mile is 4,977 pounds of the 71,294 supported annually or about 9% of the biomass. The figure for Nairobi Park is maximal, since it harbors the highest density of cheetahs. Surely the biomass transfer is only a fraction of the park estimates in most areas of the cheetah's range. This plus the selection of infirm, old, and young prey should discourage killing of cheetahs in game ranching. Economic losses from predation can be counterbalanced by tourist income from photography of cheetahs in the game ranch.

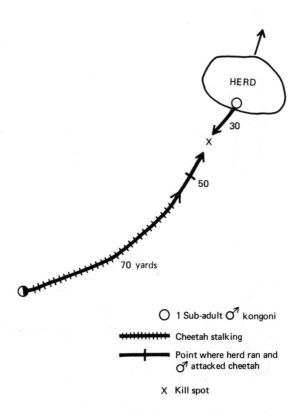

Figure 3–10 Two adult males stalked a herd of kongoni. The cheetahs were sighted and the kongonis took flight except one close kongoni, a sub-adult male, which charged the cheetahs and was killed.

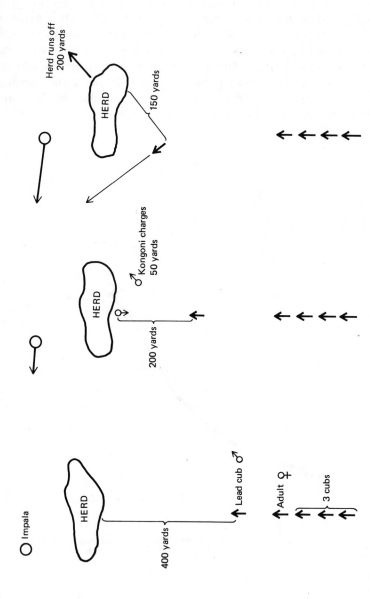

Figure 3–11 The entire cheetah family stalked a distant herd of mixed antelope. The lead cub, a nearly adult male, ran ahead of the other cheetahs, straight at the herd. As he got closer a male kongoni charged and a lone impala behind the herd took flight. As the mixed herd ran off the cheetah changed its direction of attack and pursued the impala but could not overtake it. The other cheetahs remained stationary during the attack.

COMPETITION WITH OTHER PREDATORS

To date there has been little intensive analysis of possible competitive interactions among the primary carnivores. There are data on the food habits of these top predators and Bourlieve (1963) has asked the question, how do the carnivores ". . . avoid coming into competition with one another and how can the closely related species . . . remain ecologically isolated though geographically living side by side?" It could be stated that competition does occur between coexisting species, the degree of which is measured by the impact one species has on another, that is, what would happen to the population of species A if species B were removed from the same area?

Actually very little field work has been done with competition and coexistence in natural communities. Nor do we have any real notions of how different is different enough. To evaluate the competition between predators it is important to know the segregation into habitats, age, and condition of their respective prey diets. A basis for an initial indication of competition is a test of overlap between species for their requirements. Horn (1966) has developed a useful index of overlap for ecologists. I have applied this index to available data on the prey animals taken by the lion, leopard, and cheetah in East Africa (Table 3–17).

Bourliere (1963) explained this high level of competition by pointing out

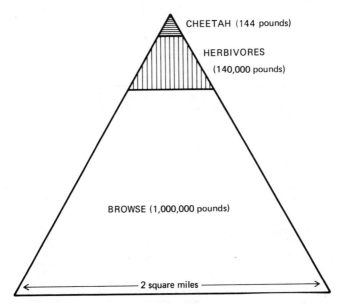

Figure 3–12   Pyramid of biomass in Nairobi National Park based on maximum estimates of cheetah density.

that the cheetah hunts in the open plains and the leopard in the riverine bush, and in different ways, the cheetah by running its prey down and the leopard by waiting and usually pouncing from a tree onto its prey. This explanation does not solve the problem. The question that now needs to be answered is, how do these two ways of living as a predator allow coexistence if there is competition for the same limited natural resources? More specifically do the cheetah and leopard really live off the same populations of ungulate prey or are they extracting different classes (age,

TABLE 3-17   THE INDEX OF OVERLAP (HORN, 1966)
AS APPLIED TO WRIGHT'S DATA FROM
NAIROBI NATIONAL PARK, 1960

Food	Lion	Leopard
Thomson's gazelle	.10	.50
Wildebeest	.49	.14
Impala	.03	.14
Zebra	.15	.07
Baboon	.00	.07
Wild dog	.00	.07
Giraffe	.04	.00
Grant's gazelle	.00	.00
Buffalo	.05	.00
Kongoni	.02	.00
(Others)	.12	.00
	1.00	1.00

$$\text{Overlap} = \frac{\sum\limits_{i=1}^{S} X_iY_i}{\sum\limits_{i=1}^{s} X_i^2 + \sum\limits_{i=1}^{s} Y_i^2} = .20$$

The results of the lion-leopard overlap test is what is normally expected with predators in the same trophic level. However, note the leopard-cheetah overlap:

Food	Leopard	Cheetah
Thomson's gazelle	.50	.58
Wildebeest	.14	.09
Impala	.14	.25
Zebra	.07	.00
Baboon	.07	.00
Wild dog	.07	.00
Reed buck	.00	.00
Grant's gazelle	.00	.09
	1.00	1.00

Overlap = .75

From 407 Observations (407) by Brynard and Pienaar, Kruger National Park during 1958–59 (Bourliere, 1963).

sex, condition, etc.) of individuals of the same species? Perhaps with the impala, for example, the cheetah visually locates a slower or less wary animal to attack while the leopard from the tree above picks out prey only on the basis of what happens to pass close enough for a kill.

To investigate this problem one has to determine the energy budgets or the energy gains and energy costs that make these two systems workable. Such a study would have to compare the cheetah system with the leopard system by evaluating each predator with respect to the following:

1. The effectiveness of the method of hunting.
2. The habitat visitation of prey to the predator's area.
3. The makeup of the prey animals in relation to their herds.

For each predator, observations of the hunting success tallied against attempted kills and the relationship of this ratio to the density of prey species have to be made. Also comparisons of biomass killed and utilized provide the data necessary for measuring competitive impact.

In comparing the ways of living found in the cheetah and leopard, for example the bioeconomics of each predator is not complete with a compilation of data from kills. Just as important in attempting to evaluate the interactions between the leopard and cheetah is the measure of visitation of suitable prey animals to each predator's domain. There are two questions inherent in this problem: (1) What constitutes a suitable prey animal, and (2) How available are prey animals to each predator in its respective habitat? Some information on the first problem is obtained by examining prey once it is attacked and killed by the predator. The second question can be answered by measuring whether or not certain animals spend more time than others in each of the predator's areas. The habitat segregation of prey animals in a leopard's or cheetah's hunting area would be compared with the attempted and actual kills of each. A longer-term study of several predators in one area, such as Schaller's (1972) study, will bring us closer to an understanding of 1 and 2; however, no field investigation has yet adequately evaluated 3 relative to concomitant predation by several predators.

INTERACTIONS OF CHEETAH WITH OTHER SPECIES

The alerting by prey of other prey was mentioned above, as was the "mobbing" response of prey. Several species, typically not prey, were responsible for such alerts, including giraffe (*Giraffa camelopardalis*), crowned cranes and species of bobos. The giraffe simply fixated on the cheetah visually and the prey species in the area responded by looking for a predator. Crowned cranes, when seeing a cheetah, honked and hovered overhead, sometimes swooping down and even lighting nearby. These activities brought the prey's attention to the cheetah.

Lions, when hunting the same prey as cheetah, caused the cheetah to stop and move away. The mere presence or even sound of lions often resulted in cheetah changing their activities and moving away from the lions.

The normal interaction between two predators occurred when the jackals hunted in the late afternoon and came onto a group of cheetahs. The jackals, often four or five, were normally spread out over several hundred yards and maintained contact by barking as they moved. When cheetahs were encountered by one of the jackals, it barked to the others and they all came to the cheetahs, sniffing the air as they approached, apparently looking for a kill. If the cheetahs were not on a kill, the jackals searched the immediate area looking for a carcass that might have just been left by the cheetahs. If nothing was found, they remained near the cheetahs for some time, following them as they moved; and when a kill was made the jackals fed on the leftover carcass. If the cheetahs had already fed and were inactive and if a carcass was not found nearby, the jackals moved on.

In November, 1966, one area of the park was often frequented by a female cheetah with four cubs (group 1) and was also the territory of a pair of jackals with three pups. The jackal young remained at the den while the adults hunted either singly or together. Upon encountering the cheetah family, the jackals approached to about 20 yards and barked but were ignored except for an occasional chase by the cubs. The jackals ran back and forth barking between the cheetahs and a herd of Grant's gazelles feeding nearby. The two jackals had gone on to hunt and were almost out of sight by the time the adult cheetah attacked two male Grant's gazelles that had grazed away from the herd. The hunt was not successful. The jackals took notice of the chase and returned to look for a kill; it appeared that they associated food with the presence of the cheetahs and perhaps with the chase.

One month later, while observing the same cheetah family, I noticed that the entire jackal family was hunting as a group. The cheetah and her cubs were about 300 yards from a herd of mixed species. This same herd had earlier spotted the cheetahs and given alarm calls. The adult cheetah was too far away for an attack, there was little or no stalking cover, and the herd was aware of her presence. The cheetahs had been lying in the shade for about half an hour since the herd spotted them when the jackals arrived. Upon discovering the cheetahs lying under an *Acacia* tree, one of the adult jackals barked until the others were congregated around the cheetah family. The jackal that had found the cheetahs crawled to within ten feet of the adult cheetah which did not respond. The jackal then stood up and made a very pneumatic sound by forcing air out of the lungs in short stacatto bursts. This same jackal turned toward the game herd, ran to it and, upon reaching it, ran back and forth barking. The individuals of the herd watched the jackal intently. The cheetah sat up and watched the hèrd as soon as it became preoccupied with the activity of the jackal. Then the cheetah quickly got up and ran at half-speed toward the herd, getting to within 100 yards before being seen by the herd. The prey animals then took flight while the cheetah pursued an impala at full speed.

Upon catching the impala and making the kill, the cheetah called to its cubs to come and eat. After the cheetahs had eaten their fill and moved away from the carcass, the waiting jackals fed on the remains.

In six other hunts a jackal from this same family was observed facilitating the stalk of the adult cheetah and one kill was made. Of 108 hunts alone the cheetah was successful 15 times giving a hunt-to-kill ratio of about 7:1; while, with the aid of jackals, the cheetah was successful 2 times during the 7 hunts giving a ratio of 3.5:1.

In most areas, other than Nairobi Park, where cheetahs and jackals are both found, the jackals do not wait for a predator to leave their kill but rather attempt to take what they can before the predator abandons the carcass. In fact, the competition between predators and scavengers is often keen (Estes, 1967). In Nairobi Park hyena (*Crocuta crocuta*) are rare and wild dog (*Lycaon pictus*) are not seen. Apparently this is the reason the jackals lack competition for the cheetahs' kills.

There seems to be no other explanation for the behavior of the jackals and cheetahs except that it is a case of interspecific cooperation in which both benefit. It is doubtful that this phenomenon is widespread between these two species; it appears to be a learned behavior characteristic of a few individuals.

It is conceivable that these two families learned to cooperate during the month interceding my first and second observations of interaction between them. It is tenable that on some occasion while the adult cheetah was near a herd, and probably hunting, one or several of the jackals were moving through the same herd and barking, as they frequently do. Consequently, the jackals distracted the herd and enabled the cheetah to attack and probably make a kill.

The fate of this learned trait probably depends on the survival of the jackals. The behavior is not likely to spread since the competition between scavengers in most areas is too keen to allow it. It is also unlikely that the cheetahs could perpetuate the behavior to other jackals since it was the scavenging habits of the jackal that made possible the interaction in the first place.

The importance of the dog (*Canis familiaris*) in the evolution of modern man and in the survival of many living cultures has long been recognized. Speculation based on fossils of dogs in stone age middens have placed the domestication of the dog at least 10,000 years ago. One common view held by many anthropologists is that when man settled down to an agrarian way of life, wild canids, long dependent on scavenging from the refuse of nomadic hunters, caught up with man, figuratively speaking, and were domesticated (Downs, 1948). The usual reasons that are offered for domestication of the dog are: for an alarm system, to rid of refuse and pests, for warmth and as a pet (Downs, 1948; Montagu, 1942).

It has been proposed that man and dog, both of which have great social affinities (Woolpy and Ginsburg, 1967), learned to cooperate in hunting (Zeuner, 1954). Just how this cooperation developed is only speculative, but evidence from hunting symbiosis in primitive peoples with their canids and between predator species is enlightening.

Several living primitive cultures that are not agrarian strongly depend for survival on their association with dogs. Aboriginies apparently brought the dingo with them to Australia and use them for hunting larger game as well as for warmth and to give warnings (Meggitt, 1961). To the bushmen of the Kalahari in South Africa their bushdogs are invaluable for hunting (Dart, 1965). The Ituri pygmies live closely with a dog species, the basenji, which shows little relationship with modern dog breeds domesticated from the wolf (*Canis lupus*) (Scott and Fuller, 1965). The basenji is avocal and cooperates in hunting in the forest. It is possible, at least in the case of the pygmies, that these cultures have domesticated canids quite independently of domestication in the Northern Hemisphere, which is considered by many to be the origin of domestication. The hunting symbioses in these three cultures is mutualistic in that in return for tracking, running, and holding the game at bay, the dogs get the offal when the prey is killed by the men with their weapons. In a sense these cases are opportunistic exploitations of dogs by man, but it is equally probable that the percent of kills made cooperatively by the two species is higher than would be possible by either species hunting alone (Downs, 1948).

If cheetah and jackal can learn to hunt mutually then it is to be expected that man's presence for hundreds of thousands of years in areas with scavenging canines would have led to cooperative hunting between the two. In fact, it is hard to believe otherwise. It is equally possible that it was man who scavenged the canid and thereby established a symbiosis. Perhaps this symbiosis facilitated the learning of effective social hunting by hominids. Selection may have favored just such an interspecific cooperation.

Agriculture probably ended the importance of hunting as the binding force between man and dog and sponsored the more intensive artificial selection of breeds for various uses. It is possible that until this period men lived closely with canids that in fossil form are indistinguishable from wild stock (Zeuner, 1954).

Domestication may have occurred through both hunting symbiosis and agricultural life; however, a hunting relationship probably led to the first domestication. Fossil evidence may eventually reconstruct behavioral associations between early man and canids. Such evidence may further dilineate the evolutionary line of the predatory *Australopithecus pithecus* from *Australopithecus robustus*.

4 Social Organization and Spacing

The female cheetah and her four nearly adult cubs were lying on a rock outcropping near the Athi River. The family group was one of four groups that reside in Nairobi National Park, an area of only 44 square miles. The male cub that had taken over leadership of the entire family approached his mother and smelled the ground where she was sitting. The male started to mount his mother but she swatted him on the head. He turned his head away, chirped like a bird, and walked back to where he was lying.

The adult female was in heat but it was eight months later that she gave birth to a second litter. The first litter gradually separated from her as she became reluctant to follow over the succeeding three months. The female had succeeded in isolating herself.

This family group and the other adult groups, composed mostly of males, frequently used the same areas of the park for hunting. However, they never came into close contact. Their paths often crossed but not less than one day apart. I came to learn that the scent markings left by frequent urination act as warnings. As one group moves along it stops at trees and rocks, marks the objects with a small amount of urine and scent, then moves on. Another group that comes along the same path smells the first group's scent and responds by going in a different direction.

Members of one group do not socialize with individuals of other groups except for mating. The female drops scent when she comes into heat and male groups follow the scent trail, mating with the female when they find her. Within one group or between groups I observed aggression only once—the mother swatting the male cub that tried to mate with her. Cheetahs do not compete at a kill site. All of them feed in peace, quite unlike lions, which squabble and fight incessantly over food.

It perplexed me that cheetahs were so peaceable compared with other members of the cat family. Their spacing behavior would imply that they actively avoided each other, but were the scent warnings backed up with the threat of actual physical aggression? Should scent markings be considered warnings?

The majority of the data on social organization are observations of the 15 cheetah of four social groups in Nairobi Park.

These cheetah were all seen in the northwest section of the park, an area of about eight square miles, within 48-hour periods on several occasions. Paths of one group often crossed the paths of other groups. Groups occasionally came into sight of one another, but actual intergroup association was not observed.

Extensive observations of groups 2, 3, and 4 showed that one male led each group. This individual determined the direction of movement, when the group hunted, and what was hunted, and was also more wary of humans, lions, and suspected danger. The leadership of group 2 was by the adult mother of the other four in November, when the cubs were three-quarters grown, at about 12 months of age. In December one of the three male cubs shared leadership with the mother, and in January, at 14 months of age and apparent sexual maturity, was the sole leader of the group. This male was more active and aggressive in play before, during, and after he became the leader. No overt physical fight was observed in his assuming leadership. In February, however, the mother came into estrus and she did exhibit aggression by hissing and slapping with her front paws at the young male when he attempted to mount her, the only aggression I observed in the wild. Early-morning and late-evening play-fights and chases were common in all groups.

Individuals seldom joined or left groups 1, 2, 3, and 4. Only group 3, the two males, separated temporarily but rejoined. Nairobi Park records and several individuals' photographs show that these two males originally hunted with two others for at least two years prior to the study, and they, too, broke up several times and rejoined.

Male cheetah are capable of directional urination as observed for tigers and lions (Schaller, 1967:251–253). The penis can be directed with accuracy at objects above or below the body (Fig. 4–1). Males in adult groups or singly pass small quantities of urine throughout the day on many objects, while females appear to urinate heavily only occasionally as a purely excretory function. Female tigers and lions (Schaller, 1967:252) emit wide

Figure 4–1   Adult male cheetah depositing scented urine on tree trunk. (Photo: H. Patel.)

sprays quite frequently. Both sexes in a cheetah group took great interest in the urination previously made by males of other groups (Fig. 4–2). Where one group marked, another group inspected and then marked the same place. The female with cubs took great interest in the markings of all other groups, and so did the cubs. Male cubs of group 1, ages 4–8 months over the study, were not observed to mark. The young males of group 2 marked at 14 months.

Places that were marked were usually objects that stood out from the immediate environment such as large trees and shrubs, dirt mounds, or concrete road embankments. In very open areas markings were made on plants that stood out against a homogeneous background of more common plants. For example thorn-tree (*Acacia drepanalobium*) makes up at least 80% of the small trees on the plains of Nairobi Park, yet *Balanites glabra,* which is much less common but usually fuller and larger, is the most commonly marked. If the *A. drepanalobium* is large or the only plant nearby, it is marked. In one area in the south end of the park three 20 ft high *Acacia mellifera* are surrounded on all sides by many *A. drepanalo-bium* but only the *A. mellifera* are marked when cheetah pass through that vicinity. Even a nonwoody plant that is different in shape or foliage from surrounding plants is a preferred marking place. Walker (1964:1282) considered these trees scratching posts; however, this is doubtful since scratching was rarely observed and may have been just stretching. Only group 3 exhibited the behavior described in tigers by Schaller (1967:254), in which the two males, after smelling and marking a frequently marked tree, scraped the grass and earth alternately with their hind legs. When the ground was bare they defecated only a small amount and/or urinated onto the scrape.

Hunting success of cheetah apparently depends mainly on vision, and little, if any, on smell, yet much time is expended smelling for, locating, and marking other markings (Table 4–1). Some objects in the home range are recognized by cheetah to be habitual marking sites. These marking locations are well known and each group orients its movements to these locations wherever it is traveling, often following a zig-zagged path between certain trees. When in one area, a group's path often followed,

Figure 4–2 Cheetah inspecting tree for olfactory markings. (Photo: H. Patel.)

TABLE 4–1 BEHAVIOR OF ADULT GROUP OF TWO MALES,
NOVEMBER 30, 1966, NAIROBI NATIONAL PARK

Time (A.M.)	Behavior
6:00	Moving east to west from evening bed
6:02	Smell then urine-mark large rock
6:05	Smell then urine-mark *Acacia*
6:07	Smell then urine-mark *Acacia*
6:10	Observe impala
6:15	Smell urine-mark large *Acacia*
6:20	Mutual face licking
6:30	Change directions, south to north (wind blowing to southwest)
6:32	Change directions towards lone female Grant's gazelle; she sees them, cheetahs stop stalking
6:33	Stop, look about for game
6:34	Stop, look about for game
6:35	Stop on small hill, look for game
6:36	Smell urine-mark 10 ft high *Balanites*, defecate on ground, scrape ground with hind legs
6:40	Female Grant's gazelle gives warning call, "snorts," at 5 sec intervals
6:41	Change directions, due east toward 15 ft high *Balanites*
6:42	Smell urine-mark *Balanites*
6:50–7:00	Watch adult male kongoni 350 yards away, stalk via vegetation at right angle to kongoni
7:01	Now 200 yards from kongoni, are discovered, lose interest, move on
7:04	Walk toward large *Acacia drepanalobium*, urine-mark it
7:06	Cross road, walking toward 20 ft high dirt mound near new dam
7:11–7:15	On mound smell top and side areas extensively, kneeling while smelling other group's markings made yesterday
7:20	Sit on mound, observe nearby herds
7:47	Male #2 defecates on mound
7:50	Move north off mound toward herds, same direction as family group moved yesterday
7:52	Mark 8 ft high *Balanites*
7:53	Male urine-marks *Balanites*
7:55	Both urine-mark concrete embankment
7:56	Drink
8:00	#2 male only urine-marks *Balanites*
8:02	On hill overlooking herds of kongoni, Grant's gazelle, and wildebeest
8:04	Both urine-mark *Balanites* after smelling it
8:05	Intent on 5 young kongoni straying from herd, no cover between cheetah and kongoni

TABLE 4-1   (continued)

Time (A.M.)	Behavior
8:09	Move off hill away from herds, west, #2 male urine-marks *Balanites*
8:15	Lie down in high grass, occasionally look at herds
9:35	Move to shade of *Balanites*
9:55	Still in shade, inactive

more or less, the same route of marking spots used before by it and other groups (Fig. 4–3).

Cheetah groups did not follow a route taken by another group on the same day; however, one group often followed in the same direction a path taken by another group on the day before (Fig. 4–3). On 14 occasions, a second group moved along another group's marking path from the day before. The distance between markings varies with the density of the woody plants, averaging about 30–50 yards in dense cover and about 50–100 yards or more in the more open plains. Of these 14 occasions, the second group followed at least 6 markings of the first group and as many as 21 with an average of 11. In no cases did the second group overtake or come into sight of the first group.

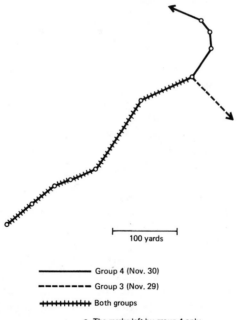

100 yards

———————— Group 4 (Nov. 30)

-------- Group 3 (Nov. 29)

++++++++++ Both groups

o The marks left by group 4 only

Figure 4–3   Paths and markings of two cheetah groups on two consecutive days.

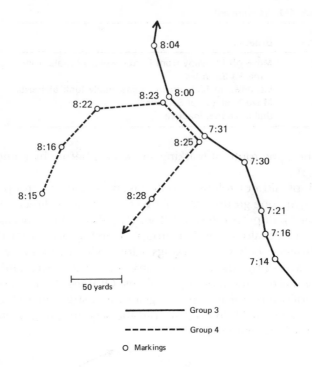

Figure 4–4 Paths of two groups on the same day.

On nine occasions a second group came upon another group's markings made on the same day. The second group was deliberate in locating and smelling other nearby markings before going on in a different direction from the first group (Fig. 4–4). The second group would spread out from where the first fresh marking was found until a second one had been located. The first animal to find another marking would kneel down and smell the scent carefully. Upon seeing one cheetah kneeling the others of the group came to where he was and behaved similarly (Fig. 4–5). After all group members took great notice of the second-found marking, the group, while marking, moved off slowly and warily in a direction different from the first group.

On five occasions two all-adult groups noticed each other while passing in opposite directions at 100–300 yards apart. Twice two groups passed within 200 yards of each other, but the vegetation prevented them from seeing each other. It should be noted here that once group 1 walked in front of a male lion only 20 yards away, and the lion watched the cheetah but the cheetah were not aware of him. The expressions that cheetah

Figure 4–5 Two male cheetahs, brothers, inspecting for the urine markings of other cheetahs on a hill in Nairobi National Park. (Photo: R. L. Eaton.)

make as group passes group fit closely the threatening behavior of other felines. In the cheetah the ears are drawn back, the head is held low and the mouth is open. In the observation of two male cheetah approaching each other on opposite ridges about 100 yards apart, yelping and marking (J. B. Foster, pers. comm.) were frequent. The two males did not meet and nothing came of the confrontation. Dogs mark in sight of each other when neither is motivated to fight (Lorenz, 1966). Group 1 when bedded down for the evening saw group 4 moving into high grass and bedding down for the night about 250 yards off. The female got up immediately and moved in the opposite direction from the three adult cheetah. She constantly turned around and looked in the direction of the other group before settling down again a mile away from the first bed site.

The absence of movement between cheetah groups indicates that members make up families. New groups are probably established as females leave a group to give birth and raise young. It is not known if females whose cubs are lost in some way reenter their old groups or simply live alone until in estrus again, but Schaller (1972) believes they remain solitary. The first possibility is supported by the fact that in a few groups, individuals left and rejoined after as long as two months. The second suggestion is supported by the fact that in some areas, cheetah are predominantly seen singly or in twos. If there were an affinity for groups to admit foreign individuals or for single animals to join, then most cheetah sightings in these areas would be of groups, but they are not. That markings may serve to get broken-up groups back together is ostensible; however, markings do not appear to serve as a means of enabling a foreign cheetah to locate and become a member in an established group.

Predation on cheetah cubs may act as a regulatory mechanism that consequently keeps populations too low to allow natural selection for a spacing mechanism that is limiting. Apparently population control in wolves results from cub mortality (Rausch, 1967) and social castration (Woolpy, 1968). That predation may be more important in controlling numbers than territoriality is shown, for example, in muskrats (*Ondatra zibethecus*). Errington (1963:71) holds predation as relatively unimportant, but the fact that muskrat territories become compressed as density increases implies that territory cannot be acting as the only factor in regulating muskrat populations. Lions, unlike cheetah, are well known for their aggressive behavior to outsiders. The evolution of "baby-sitting" (Schaller, 1972) has decreased the problem of predation to lion cubs and of course has reproductive value (Slobodkin, 1961:51). Since predation is not an appreciable factor in lions, it is likely that a spacing system dependent on marking and other mechanisms is more important in limiting populations of lions than of cheetah. Aggression is also more important in the lion—nonpride members or territorial intruders may be killed (Schenkel, 1966, 1967, Eaton 1973).

It is worthy of speculation that aggression within the pride and toward outsiders might vary over long-term cycles of game abundance depending on the pride's size. The optimum pride size is bound to depend on game abundance levels, and levels of aggression are probably built in to compensate for reaching this optimal pride size, for example in a period of game abundance a small pride would increase in size due to a lowered level of aggression within the pride and toward strangers, a large pride would probably not alter its aggression level. Conversely, with game scarcity the small pride, being nearer an optimal size, would be at an advantage to drive off or kill strange lions that attempted to enter the group, and a large pride could be reduced toward the "best" pride size by increased levels of aggression. Also, since lions probably have a relatively long reproductive life, cubs could be kept away from kills and starved to death in order for the pride to survive through the low part of a game cycle (which is related to the approximate five year rainfall cycle in East Africa [Talbot and Talbot, 1963].

Since members of lion prides often separate for periods while hunting (Schaller, 1972), marking could be functional in getting members together, for example to share a kill or for cooperative hunting efforts. Cheetah groups, on the other hand, seldom have members leaving with the probable exception of females for breeding activities. The functions of marking in cheetah probably do not include a means for an individual to locàte the group or vice-versa although this possibility appears likely for certain canids and possibly the tiger. Many animals use markings to communicate estrus condition (Bourliere, 1954). The cheetah female when in estrus does pass scent that is of interest to males wherever she sits or urinates; however, except during estrus, urination appears to occupy chiefly an excretory function. For lions, tigers, and house cats vocalizations may act as important mating cues. Cheetahs also appear to vocalize to attract mates.

The facial expressions of cheetah when two groups pass are typical threatening gestures. When threat behaviors are well established it is to be expected that aggression between social groups is relatively rare. Only two observed cases of overt aggression in wild cheetah (Stevenson-Hamilton, 1947) indicate that the cheetah has a system that reduces the number of aggressive encounters. It is efficient in that strangers rarely meet.

The attention that cheetah give to markings indicates that there is information transfer between cheetahs. Since cheetah groups do not associate but do notice one another's markings, then at least part of the message must be a warning.

Female tigers and lions do mark (Schaller, 1967), but female cheetahs apparently do not. Social evolution in the tiger has probably led to a need for the female to mark; however, that the degree of specialization has been limited by the female's anatomy is shown by the female's less efficient wide spray as opposed to the finer emission of males.

The male provides the chemical warnings just as in many species of birds and mammals defense of territories is only by the males. A female with cubs does not associate with adult males and therefore may lack a chemical warning system. Perhaps females with young are not spaced. According to Lorenz (1966:43), "Where only one sex cares for the brood, only that sex is really aggressive toward members of the species." It is possible that females with cubs, as in dogs, receive a "higher respect" from other adults. Regardless, the female does heed other groups' markings and moves away from another group when they are sighted, thus remaining spaced.

The cheetah groups in the study area avoided contact with each other, in spite of the relative crowding in one small area. When another group was seen, contact was not made and threat behaviors appear to function in this regard. If chemical warnings were for a fixed-area territorial scheme then they were not effective, for the groups crossed marking paths constantly. The frequent marking of a route taken by cheetah probably serves as a means to prevent other groups from stumbling onto them and interfering with their hunting, and the possibility of aggression from the encounter. The marking must be a chemical message capable, no doubt, of losing its information content over time by dissipation. In this way, the warning is good only when needed. The markings are noticed a day after they are made, and later, but they are not respected. They probably have lost their warning intensity level.

The minimum time observed in the field after which one group would follow in the same direction on the same path as another group was 24 hours. Since cheetah are diurnal and normally active only from 5:30 A.M. to 7:00 P.M., the earliest marking made on one day would still be in effect up to the same time on the following day. This system may be facilitated by the fact that cheetah are constantly moving, and when so doing, they mark. Often these moves are just short distances, at the longest every few hours, such as at mid-day, but it apparently serves to guarantee that a group's last marking will still be in effect.

In thinking about spacing systems in cheetah it is helpful to ask why a fixed-area territory is not found. Brown (1964) uses this approach with birds but the ideas in general are applicable. To maintain an exclusive territory is often advantageous, but for such a system to evolve, territories must be biologically economical. The organism must be able to exclude intruders at a time and energy expense that is practical. If the costs of defense are too great then the advantages are not sufficient to counterbalance them.

With the cheetah it can be asked, "Could the cheetah conceivably defend an exclusive territory?" The answer is probably no. The space or area needed by a group is too large for constant patrolling without complete disruption of the group's hunting. Therefore, however advantageous it might be for a group to have an exclusive hunting area there is probably no way of maintaining such an area. If the presence of one group tends to cause another group to move elsewhere, then natural selection would favor any behavioral patterns that would more clearly indicate the presence of the group. Thus marking behavior can be expected to evolve, and this may come to have significant impact on the distribution of groups. Within groups, marking may have significance as an act of dominance.

I prefer to conceptualize this spacing mechanism as a moving territory that is maintained by markings that constitute temporary boundaries.

All of the following observations indicate that an intraspecific spacing mechanism which is territorial in nature is acting in the cheetah: (1) cheetah are highly specialized anatomically for marking, which they do frequently; (2) cheetah examine closely the markings made by other cheetah; (3) 15 cheetah belonging to four social groups were frequently seen in the same area at nearly the same time without meeting or associating even when in sight of one another; and (4) cheetah alter their direction of movement when they encounter fresh markings of other cheetah, but do not if the other group's markings are a day old.

A similar spacing system is described for the house cat by Leyhausen and Wolff (1959). Many cats use the same set of paths in their overlapping home ranges, but isolation is accomplished by frequent urine-marking as each cat moves along a trail. Any other cat that encounters a mark will stop, look ahead and possibly wait, or will head down a different, unoccupied route.

RESPONSE TO MARKS: CAPTIVE STUDIES

At Lion Country Safari and World Wildlife Safari I was able to learn more about marking behavior and its probable role in spacing, and to compare cheetahs to lions. A comparison of lion and cheetah in their response to marks of urine and feces is provided in Table 4–2.

TABLE 4–2 COMPARISON OF MARKING BEHAVIOR AND RESPONSES TO MARKS IN CHEETAH AND LION

	Cheetah		Lion	
	Male	Female	Male	Female
Tail-up marking:				
with scraping	X	—	X	X
with treading	X	—	—	—
Rear-end down:				
marking	—	X	X	X
urination	X	X	X	X
with scraping	X	—	X	X

Inspected by:	Cheetah		Lion	
	Male	Female	Male	Female
Tail-up markings of:				
male	X	X	X	X
female	n.a.[a]	n.a.	X	X
Rear-end down markings of:				
male	—	—	X	X
female	X	—	X	X

	Cheetah		Lion	
	Male	Female	Male	Female
Scraping with defecation	X	—	—	—
Olfactory inspection of feces	X	X	—	—

n.a. = not applicable.

Figure 4–6   The Fehmen response in the lion is highly exaggerated and pronounced. (Photo: R. L. Eaton.)

Although male lions mark more frequently than females and respond to a proestrous female's urine with more *Flehmen* responses than other females, both sexes do exhibit the same spectrum of response to marks and urine. The actual motor patterns of *Flehmen*, and postures of marking and urination are the same in both sexes. The differences are purely quantitative in degree of intensity, that is, frequency of occurrence.

Cheetahs of both sexes display *Flehmen* identically, but it has been observed less frequently in females in response to marks. Males and females exhibit the same frequencies of *Flehmen* to dummy cheetahs, human urine, and novel objects or odors, for example antiseptic spray on other cheetahs.

Exactly why the motor patterns of the *Flehmen* response are so strikingly different in cheetah and lion is not known, unless the more elaborate expression in the lion acts as a visual releaser (Fig. 4–6). On many occasions a lion exhibited *Flehmen* and thereby attracted others to him, whereupon they inspected the same urine marking and also showed *Flehmen.* In these cases the other lions were up to 50 meters or more away and appeared to be responding visually to the *Flehmen* expression.

Lions take odors both from the air and by extending the tongue to touch and pick up the odiferous substance before eliciting *Flehmen.* Cheetahs acquire airborne and surface-bound chemicals also prior to *Flehmen;* however, there is a difference in the motor patterns involving the tongue.

The lion's tongue is extended straight outwards and brought back into the oral cavity. The movement is rapid and only the very tip of the tongue contacts the surface. The cheetah's tongue is used in a lapping type movement in which a large portion of the dorsal surface of the tongue comes into contact with the surface.

DEFECATION AND RESPONSE TO FECES

Cheetahs lack the sanitary control found in lions. They defecate on tops of logs, rocks, or simply in the shady areas where they lie up (Fig. 4–7). The lions at Lion Country Safari get up, walk away from the lying-up area of the pride, and defecate. Cheetahs are adapted for a near-constant rate of travel around their home range and selection has not acted to bring about the sanitary habit found in lions, which frequently use the same resting spots or remain sedentary for longer periods of time. Consequently, at Lion Country Safari, with wide-ranging movements artificially inhibited, cheetah feces are highly concentrated at resting spots.

Feces conceivably could carry scent and act as markings. Cheetahs are known to inspect feces and have been observed in the wild to scrape with the hind feet when defecating, which implies feces may carry olfactory information. Lions are, like cheetahs, social, but show no response to feces.

The explanation for difference in response to feces in lions and cheetahs relies on our knowledge of their spacing behavior in the wild. Cheetahs move much more from day to day around their home range, and unlike lions, they do not have a more-or-less fixed geographic territory. Instead, cheetahs employ a time-plan spacing system which allows several groups or individuals to occupy the same home range concomitantly, without disruption of hunting efforts. The system is effective because fresh markings are responded to as warnings and the course of direction is changed. Scraping, though rarely associated with defecation, may be responded to visually. Observation of scraping in the wild and the inspection of feces by cheetahs at Lion Country Safari implies that defecation also plays a role in spacing, or at least is communicative.

Lions rarely exhibit scraping with defecation, and I have never seen them inspect feces. In fact, I have introduced the fresh feces of foreign lions to the lions of another pride, at times only inches from the nose, and there was no inspection. In the defense of a large territory, the deposition of feces would hardly be important compared with the highly efficient use of small amounts of urine.

In the cheetah system of spacing, maximized marking would be expected since exact territorial boundaries do not exist and cannot become well known to foreign individuals. There is a greater probability of one cheetah group not being aware of another's whereabouts. For this reason, defecation has evolved as an additional spacing mechanism in cheetahs.

In the way of summary of information available that is pertinent to spacing systems in the cat family, Table 4–3 is provided. It can be seen that there are correlations in these data which begin to tell us more about the "whys" of spacing differences and similarities across several species.

Several species—cougar, tiger, leopard, lynx, bobcat, and serval—lead a relatively solitary way of life. They all live in forest and/or forest edge habitats that produce far less biomass of terrestrial prey than the more open savanna and grassland plains. These species cannot afford to live in social groups. The smaller species, for example lynx, bobcat, and serval, kill prey smaller than themselves, which could not adequately feed several adults. Furthermore, several individuals hunting together would be less effective, in that they would create more disturbance and frighten off prey.

In their evolution, the cats specialized primarily in stealth and stalking to capture prey, quite unlike the dog family, in which the prey is typically

Figure 4–7 Cheetah inspecting feces on top of a log. (Photo: R. L. Eaton.)

TABLE 4-3 SUMMARY OF INFORMATION RELEVANT TO SPACING SYSTEMS[a]

Animal	Habitat Preference	Social Organization	Home Range Size (Square Miles)	Spacing Mechanisms (M = Male; F = Female)	Source
Cougar	Forest, scrub, edge	Female and young; single adults	10–25	Urine: M, ? Feces: — Scraping: — Scratching: —	Hornocker (1969)
Tiger	Forest, edge	Female and young; single adults	10–15	Urine: M, F Feces: M, F Scrapes: M, F Vocalizations: M, F	Schaller, 1967 Singh, 1971 D. Shorey, pers. comm.
Leopard	Forest, savanna	Female and young; single adults	10–30	Urine: M, ? Scrapes: M, ? Vocalizations: M, ? Scratching: M, F	Myers, 1971; Muckenhirn and Eisenberg, 1973
Serval	Forest, edge, scrub	Female and young; single adults	?	Urine: ?, ? Scrapes: ?, ?	York, 1973
Lynx; Bobcat	Forest, edge	Female and young; single adults	12–20; 1–5	Urine: M, F Feces: F, ?	Berrie, 1973 Provost, 1973
Housecat	Open fields	Female and young; single adults	?	Urine: M, ? Scrapes: M, F	Leyhausen and Wolff, 1957
Cheetah	Open plains, savanna, open woodland	Female and young; adult groups; predominantly males, and single adults	20–50+	Urine: M, — Feces: M, F Scrapes: M, —	Eaton, 1970a
Lion	Plains, savanna, miombo woodland, montane, desert	Extended matriarchy—all sex and age classes, usually fewer adult males than females	20–100+	Urine: M, F Scrapes: M, F Vocalizations: M, F Active aggression: M	Schaller, 1969; Schenkel, 1966; Eloff, 1973; Eaton, 1973

[a] (?) = unknown; (—) = not found.

chased and run down. For most cats to be successful they must hunt alone. In less productive biotopes, such as the forest, a large cat can kill and depend on prey as large or larger than itself, but group hunting would not be any advantage. It would lead to a lower hunting success not to mention more bellies to feed. A cougar kills about one deer per week, on which it feeds for several days. An adult group of cougars would scare off disproportionately more game than they could collectively acquire for food.

For those reasons most cats are solitary, and they require a relatively large hunting area to provide adequate food resources. A fixed territory is the best way to achieve the following:

1. Hunting success—other individuals hunting in the same area would disrupt and thwart the resident's own hunting success.
2. Adequate resources—a large enough area will ensure that even during resource scarcity, an adequate population of prey is available to the territorial occupant.
3. "Prudence"—the entire predator population is thus spaced out over an area in such a way that they will not overeat their prey resources, and thereby kill off the prey and themselves.

These cats more or less defend their areas in the same way, utilizing chemical and visual warnings that communicate their presence without having to physically threaten or agress intruders. Besides, it would be impossible to keep tabs on the entire territory at the same time. Thus, other means have evolved to replace and represent the proprietor's rights and intent to defend his area against conspecifics. In all these same species we see that males are wider ranging but that females maintain more stringent boundaries against other females. This too makes sense in that a female must provide an area, and its resources, sufficiently large to feed her young without competition from other family groups. The males are at an advantage the larger the territory is. The more territories of females that can be encompassed by a male the more offspring he can procreate. It goes without saying that natural selection favors a higher reproductive success. The result is a population with fewer territorial males than there are adult males, many of which are transients and forced to "wait their turn." It can be seen why a territorial male has a territory larger than what he requires for food alone, which is the major factor determining size of female territories.

In a different biotope, the grassland plains or savanna, we find in the cats:

1. different social organizations;
2. larger home ranges; and
3. different hunting techniques.

The open areas are more productive. The density and biomass of prey are greater here; however, in this habitat, hunting in the typical cat fashion would be less effective, for the prey have better visibility. This is one reason that the cheetah evolved its fantastic specializations for great speed. There was a niche for a predator on smaller, swift antelope. The plains of Africa have a great diversity of medium and smaller sized prey species most of which are hunted by pack-living predators, for example wild dog and hyena, that employ running and/or speed more than stealth.

When the many larger ungulates evolved in the late Pleistocene, the *Panthera* group of cats also evolved, apparently as a "response" to new predatory niches. The leopard, lion, and tiger all appeared most recently in felid evolution.

The lion became the largest predator in Africa, living primarily on the plains; the tiger became largest in Asia, living primarily in its vast forested regions. The lion had few competitors for the larger African prey such as adult wildebeeste, zebra, and buffalo. Stealth is certainly used by lions to capture and kill equally large or larger prey, which feeds several lions for several days. Also employed by lions is cooperation in which one lion puts prey to flight directly toward other lions.

The availability of large prey in dense populations might itself have been conducive for early evolution of group life; however, additional factors soon become operative. The group would have to maintain a large enough area to supply game year round. The prey populations respond in terms of densities and movements to the annual cycles of rainfall and drought, so that during some periods of the year, game is relatively scarce and a larger hunting area is required. This is why lion prides often have such large territories. Defense of this area is critical not only for food resources but also to protect young since intruding male lions have no inhibition about killing and eating a pride's cubs. One other factor favoring sociality in lions is protection of cubs against the many other predators. While one female hunts and kills, another female actively babysits the cubs.

Regarding the cheetah it can be seen that where prey is abundant brothers may stay together into adulthood and be able to survive on what they kill. They tend to kill larger prey than single adults. The female must live away from other adults since the size of prey she can kill is smaller, and she must be able to feed four or five cubs for about one year. The cheetah cannot live in prides. They are unable to kill large prey, owing to specializations for speed which have reduced the cheetah's overall size, power, and killing tools—the teeth and claws.

Their specializations for a limited range of prey size and a specific hunting habitat require that the cheetah be able to cover a large area. A small group (three or four) of adults or a family could not economically defend the area required. A fixed territory is not practical, thus a spacing system has evolved which temporally separates cheetahs. It is a time-plan system with boundaries that move as the warnings lose their effect. This same pattern was seen in the Kalahari lion, which also requires an area too large to demarcate and maintain absolute boundaries. Again, this is the result of availability of prey, quite low in an arid habitat.

It has been shown that a variety of mechanisms are employed to achieve spacing in the cat family. The advantages to spacing may be food, mating, population control, or some combination of these. Regardless of the system, whether it is a fixed territory or a time-plan, or a combination, the particulars of how each species remains spaced out in the environment are understandable only in terms of "defensibility." Ability to defend an area, directly or indirectly, must be economical so that the expense of time and energy does not outweigh the advantages to the individual.

The above generalizations do not include discussion of special social classes, for example nomadic lions (Schaller, 1972). And the unusual patterns of spacing brought on by varying ecological conditions are not treated, rather, what appears to be the basic system is presented.

5 Courtship and Mating Behavior

Courtship behavior has rarely been seen in the wild, and has never been completely described or photographed. One of the values of the new environmental zoos such as San Diego Wild Animal Park, is their ability to more successfully breed rare and endangered species. Breeding programs in wildlife parks have already succeeded, not only in producing cheetahs but also in learning more about courtship and mating requirements.

At Lion Country Safari cheetahs frequently groomed each other by licking, particularly in the face, lateral neck, and shoulders (Fig. 5–1). Groups of cheetahs (up to five), male, female, and mixed, laid or sat in a star formation, all licking one another's faces simultaneously. There are certain older males to whom the young females seem attracted for grooming sessions. These males are similar in that they tend to lie-up alone. The young females were members of the same social group while the older males from whom they so often solicited grooming were not. When one young female was released from isolation in the enclosure after five days, she went from cheetah to cheetah and licked each of their faces briefly. She made her way across the entire section stopping at nearly every cheetah. It is believed that mutual grooming is socially reinforcing in the wild groups, and appears to obtain at higher levels in members of social groups still together in captivitiy at Lion Country Safari and World Wildlife Safari. Short grooming sessions after prolonged lack of interaction

Figure 5–1 Socially familiar and courting cheetahs frequently groom one another (Photo: R. L. Eaton.)

may constitute a form of inspection and identification of other cheetahs since the *Flehmen* response often follows. There does not appear to be any significant reflection of dominance or status in who grooms whom except that females often intitiated grooming with older, larger males.

Grooming of other cheetahs by females in behavioral estrus was similar in motor pattern to the social grooming described above but it differed in several significant ways (the use of the tongue is the same in both cases and usually both animals have their eyes closed). First, the female in estrus elicited the behavior much more frequently, going from male to male. Males either reciprocated by licking the female or they simply did not respond. Secondly, unlike social grooming which lasts anywhere from 5 to 30 minutes, the courtship grooming was shorter with any single male. The female either moved on to another male or more advanced stages of courtship then took place.

In the summer months, courtship grooming and all phases of courtship occurred throughout the day while social grooming was seen later in the day or following feeding. However, as winter approached and the cheetahs were more active, social grooming occurred throughout the day (S. J. Craig, pers. comm.).

Typically, it is the male that marks in the wild, and at Lion Country and World Wildlife Safari this was also the case. The usual posture is a tail-up while standing and facing 180° away from the marked object—tree, rock, stump, etc. The hind legs are raised and lowered alternately four or five times during the emission of from two to six urine jets. This treading movement (sometimes referred to as "skating") appears to have been derived from scraping behavior associated commonly with marking in other felids. Scraping movements of the hind legs were observed in wild cheetahs only rarely, and then only in males. It was observed at Lion Country only in the two oldest males.

The tail touches the marked object and the tip of the tail is moved backward and forward and laterally touching both sides of the object prior to the squirting of urine. It appears that tactile information from the tail allows proper orientation in effectively directing the urine. The cheetah does not orient visually to the marked object once its rear is turned toward the object. The same is true of lions but they do not tread extensively; instead, the scraping movement of the hind feet alternately is exhibited more commonly.

In the wild only two, older male cheetahs were observed marking in the rear-end down posture or squat. At Lion Country several males urinated in the rear-end down posture. It was seen when males ran toward an estrus female that had given the "yelp" call. The males, running from 100 yards or more away, stopped abruptly, lowered their rear ends, urinated, and scraped with their hind feet. In these cases the fluid was passed not in jets but in a steady stream. Scraping during urination (a steady flow of urine) was also exhibited by the two older males in situations unrelated to mating.

The tail-up posture markings were frequently made by cheetahs on the same objects, inspected by smelling and marked over by other cheetahs. In no cases observed did cheetahs smell at or mark over the urine passed in the rear-end down posture by a male.

Urine markings are smelled and often *Flehmen* follows. *Flehmen* in wild cheetahs was not described in my field study, I simply did not recognize it as such. After smelling a urine mark or some novel object, the cheetah raises its head to the horizontal plane, the mouth is opened 3 in. and held open for only two to three seconds. Occasionally the tongue is slowly extended and touches the odoriferous object, or, repeated, relatively slow lapping of the tongue is elicited prior to *Flehmen*. There is no raising of the lips or wrinkles in the face during *Flehmen*. Lions raise the head above the horizontal usually. In both species, smelling and *Flehmen* are often repeated and marking of the marked object may follow. My olfactory inspection of fresh markings or frequently marked objects resulted in a strong sensation. The odor is decidedly "musky."

In periods preceding or between courtship chases involving one male and one female, both sexes lick the posterior and inside, lateral surface of the upper rear legs of the other (Fig. 5–2). This is often associated with licking of the genitals and surrounding area. Licking of the hair on the hind legs is often accompanied by small biting movements with the incisors and pulling of the hair as the head is drawn backwards. *Flehmen* may follow both the hind leg licking and nipping.

Males smell the genital area of other males and of females by approaching from behind while both are walking. The male places his nose between the rear legs and below the abdomen of the cheetah walking ahead. Then the dorsal surface of the nose is raised upwards in short quick movements against the genitalia. A male following a male or female, with his head extended forward and nearly touching the rear-end of the cheetah ahead, at times exhibits an erect penis.

A male and an estrus female often stand side by side, facing opposite directions, and orient their heads laterally to each other's genitalia (Fig.

Figure 5–2 A male and female inspecting ano-genital areas. (Photo: R. L. Eaton.)

5–2). This posture is often maintained as the pair walks in a circle. Orientation by the male in smelling is to the female's mid-back dorsally, and then her genital area prior to mounting.

COURTSHIP

Courtship was highly variable in temporal patterning, and with respect to numbers of males pursuing an estrus female. The male group courtship behavior was relatively restricted to early mornings and late afternoons, and after sundown on moonlight nights. The single male and female courtships were seen at the above times but also later in the mornings and earlier in the afternoons. At World Wildlife Safari and San Diego Wild Animal Park, male group courtship did not occur. In these captive cheetahs, one male was decidedly dominant over other males, and was the primary courting male.

Associated with the courtship chases were frequent play or mock fights between the estrus female and male(s), and between the estrus female and other females. In fact, in several cases a female joined males in chasing an estrus female and also took part in the mock fights with the estrus female. The mock fights associated with play chases in courtship are typified by raising up on the hind legs and coming down with the forelegs on the "opponent." These brief encounters are often followed by chases.

In the one male–one female courtship, there is, along with the chases and as a part of the mock fights, frequent pawing and biting oriented to the scruffy, short mane on the dorsal neck. Both sexes exhibit the behavior, and estrus females direct the neck bite to other females prior to mounting and thrusting them.

During the end of a courtship chase, and prior to mounting, the male may place his open jaws over the laterodorsal neck while slowly running, walking, or standing alongside the female. The bite does not appear to be full strength, but rather highly ritualized and inhibited, as compared, for example, with the neck bite of copulation. The bite has the effect of slowing the female down and inhibits her behavior generally. Here, the female frequently responds by "flopping" or falling onto her side, which is seen in fighting contexts as a submissive gesture (Fig. 5–1).

When the female bites the male in the same way, or places one forepaw on his dorsal neck or shoulders, he too often exhibits the "flop" response. It is common at this stage for either the male or female to place one foreleg over the other's back, and around the midsection, suggestive of foreleg clasping in mounting.

The male chases the female who runs with her tail in the "tail-up" posture or the "curled over" posture. Chases are frequent and for distances of usually 50–150 yards. They end when the chased animal either actively elicits the flop response in submission, or the pursuer overtakes the pursued and places a forepaw or ritualized bite on the pursued's dorsal neck, shoulders, or midback.

At Lion Country Safari the same group of five males took part in courtship of estrus females, and though other single males not members of the group had courted and mated females, no other males than these five exhibited group courtship. The group pursuit of a female was initiated in either of two ways: (1) a single male courting or copulating a female attracted the group of males; (2) the estrus female running with the tail-curled over or tail-up posture in sight of the group. A description of the first case follows from my notes: "A male and female play-fight in a wrestle-type posture. Both are lying side by side on the ground, their stomachs facing each other. There is mutual pawing with the forelegs against the other's lateral neck and head, and occasional soft kicking with the hind legs. The male stands over the female, she is now on her back facing upwards at him. She paws his lateral neck and head with both forepaws. The female rolls over onto her stomach. The male mounts, holds the scruff of the female's neck. The female stands up quickly and runs with the tail straight up. The male chases her." The chase ends when either the female flops or simply stops and stands still. In the latter case the female turns towards the approaching males, faces them and swats them on the head. Often then the female walks slowly away with her tail up and the males follow, smelling at her rear and showing penile erection.

The female normally initiates another or several chases, followed by a flop. When she did not dart away, the five males formed a circle around the female and lay down. In a short time one male (other females may join in the chase and lie in the circle) was up and approached the estrus female, and soon another and possibly a third. A fight broke out between one of the males and the female, the female fought defensively on her back, swatting with her forelegs and kicking with her hindlegs. Soon the males were fighting amongst themselves, and the female lay nearby watching. These courtship fights were unique in that they involved so many individuals at one time (Fig. 5–3). Hundreds of fights observed and filmed in other contexts, for the most part feeding competition on a single "kill," showed not one case of more than two cheetahs involved in the same fight even when many were at close quarters.

The most intense fight, that is, with the most biting and longest duration, was observed between two males in competition for an estrus female (S. Craig, pers. comm.). In intense aggression, males exhibit the tail-under posture, similar to that of submission in canines. It is also seen during threatening of an approaching human and precedes flight. Feeding

Figure 5–3   Male cheetahs competing for mating rights of female in heat. Fights between males during courtship at Lion Country Safari, California, were the most intense expression of aggression. The great number of males present may explain the lack of a clearly established dominance rank among males, which occurred at the San Diego Wild Animal Park. (Photo: R. L. Eaton)

fights seldom involved biting while courtship fights did. Bites in food competition are highly ritualized and directed to the lateral face. Biting in courtship fights was more intense and directed to several areas. Rising up on the hindlegs and sparring with the forelegs was common in courtship, only seldom in feeding.

The female remained lying down throughout the courtship fight between males, and the other females in the "mating circle" also remained lying down. Once the fight was over, the female got up and walked away. The males smelled the ground where the female was last lying, then followed the female. It was impossible to determine which male "won" in the courtship fights, if indeed one did. It has not been apparent to date whether or not fights in group courtship affect which male actually mates the female. At the San Pasqual Wild Animal Park of the San Diego Zoo, ten cheetahs were kept in two five-acre paddocks. In one, with a group of three males and two females, one male was decidedly dominant. He was most active in courtship and was aggressive to the other males when they approach the estrus female (R. Herdman, 1973.) At Lion Country Safari no instances of such long-term absolute dominance have emerged; however, the World Wildlife Safari cheetahs behaved similarly to those at San Diego. At San Diego and World Wildlife Safari fewer cheetahs are kept in larger areas than at Lion Country Safari. The exceptionally high density of cheetahs at Lion Country is probably responsible for these differences.

Although it is generally the rule that females are submissive in courtship, or that they are aggressive only insofar as they swat pursuing males, it should be noted that in the one male–one female courtships, a female sometimes becomes quite aggressive, to the point of eliciting submissive postures in the male.

COPULATION

Copulation is the same in both the one-male and male-group courtship. In the latter, while one male copulates the female the other males of the original courting group stand or sit nearby, as close as four feet. The nonmating males show no fight or threat behavior during copulation. After copulation, no courtship was observed by the same female for about an hour, and usually not until the following early morning when a copulation occurred in the preceding evening.

The female is approached by the male. The male places his teeth on the scruff of her neck. The female, whether standing, sitting, or lying down, moves into the receptive posture—hind-end elevated by posterior placement of the hind feet under the rear end. The tail is moved laterally, the posture resembles that of the female house cat. The male places his forelegs around the female's body just behind her shoulders and grips the skin of her dorsal neck very tightly in his teeth. The male intromits and thrusts rapidly about 20–30 times in succession. The female remains motionless throughout copulation. After thrusting, the male relaxes his grip on her neck, dismounts and walks away.

As the male dismounts, the female rolls over onto her back and swats the dismounting male on the side of the head. The female then exhibits an after-response, she rolls over from side to side and remains lying down for several seconds before standing up. The other males remain around her, and she dashes away with the males chasing her. The chase is short and the female lies down, unresponsive to the males.

In testing response to mounted specimens of cheetahs, one male mounted the dummy and clasped it in the typical manner, then thrust it with an erection (fig. 5–4). The same male behaved similarly with a dummy leopard but after "mating" the cheetah, the male exhibited an extensive after-response, just like the female's, only exhibiting an erection. This was the only after-response seen in a male cheetah.

Figure 5–4 Cheetahs inspecting a mounted cheetah specimen. (Photo: R. L. Eaton.)

Figure 5–5 Cheetah calls being recorded to later observe their effects on behavior. (Photo: R. L. Eaton.)

COMPETITION FOR MATE

Females did not compete in any direct way for males when more than one was in estrus. Only two females of the six at Lion Country Safari ever came into season, the other four were either too young, or in the case of one, injured and removed and kept isolated in the enclosure. In the dummy experiments, both males and females threatened the cheetah dummy but not the leopard except by approaching it at a distance. Males and females inspected both leopard and cheetah dummies by smelling and nipping at the head and neck and at the genital area and upper, posterior hind legs—the same locations inspected on live cheetahs. After inspecting the cheetah dummy females attacked with intraspecific aggressive behavior, but the males did not. With the leopard, the females, after inspection, treated it as prey—pulling it over and immediately directing the strangle bite to the ventral throat. The males responded to the leopard as prey only after the females "killed" it, at which time the males circled around the fallen "prey" and began to lick and attempt to eat it. What is interesting is that the female cheetahs apparently recognized the dummy cheetah as a conspecific and were aggressive to it, perhaps a reflection of their less sociable nature.

At Lion Country Safari males competed directly for a female on several occasions besides the ceremonial and highly ritualized fights in the "mating circle." A single male following an estrus female attacked and fought with three or four approaching males. More frequently than actual combat was a single male staying close to a female and simply turning towards an approaching male, threatening with the open mouth, and staring directly at the male. This was sufficient to deter the potential competitor's approach.

A female lying down with a male was often approached by a second male that first smelled at her mid-dorsal back, then progressively backwards to her genital area. The male already with the female got up and faced the second male, and the second male submitted by turning his head away, then walking away. In one instance a male had been mating with and following a female all morning. The pair was lying down together away from any other cheetahs when four adult males approached them and laid down close by. The mating male threatened the four males, and immediately one of the males mounted another male. Being threatened and at the same time sexually motivated and attracted to the threatening male's mate resulted in redirected sexual bahavior to another male.

The above case was one of the three instances in which homosexual behavior was observed in males. It is reported in zoos as quite frequent, which to me indicates that something is amiss at the zoos. Often the homosexual behavior correlates with loud noises or unusual disturbances, all the more reason to believe it is an abnormal response or is indicative of frustration. A female displayed the full range of male copulatory behavior to another female when the former was in heat. She mounted and clasped with the forelegs, gripped the neck and thrust several times. The mounted female did not exhibit an after-response.

An estrus female often got up, walked away to higher ground, and gave the "chirp" or whistle call (it resembles the cheep of a chick). Immediately, all the cheetahs in sight lifted their heads and faced the female. Usually only one or two males approached a chirping female, and once there attempted to mount her without success. The chirp is heard in many contexts unrelated to mating and is made by males and females alike. When given by an estrus female it sometimes but not always attracts males. It is the same call that brings cubs to their mother in the wild. It was elicited from day of birth by a cheetah cub born at the San Pasqual Wild Animal Park, where it was removed from the mother the day it was born (R. Herdman, 1973).

The stutter call is surely derived from purring, but is also quite distinctive. It is the pitch of the purr, and consists of four to six short notes given in rapid succession, resembling the cooing of a pigeon. It is heard as cheetahs approach water or food. In mating it is heard from the female after a male attempts to mount but the female is aggressive to him. It was heard from an estrus female that was surrounded by three males. The call resulted in additional males running towards the female. When given by a male, other males pull the head away and close the eyes suggesting that the call is a warning. We played recordings of the stutter call back to the cheetahs and it elicited immediate attention and approach by all males and females (Fig. 5–5). Furthermore, it induced males to smell the genital areas of females and other males when this behavior had not been seen for several weeks.

A third call associated with courtship is the "yelp." It is high-pitched but lower than the chirp. Phonetically the yelp is "eeeow," starting at a higher pitch and ending at a lower pitch, about one-half second in duration. A female made the call and three males ran from 100 yards to where the female had been sitting and then smelled the ground and marked nearby trees without pursuing the female. Most frequently it is associated with submission.

In evenings when courtship and mating behavior were frequent, males and females both displayed behavior reminiscent of that seen in house cats with catnip, and resembling the after-response. Individually, they pushed the sides of the head, neck, and shoulders against short, two to three foot high shrubs. This resulted in lying on their sides and pawing the shrubs in that position. Rolling onto the back and moving the dorsal head laterally, rubbing it against the ground and the bent-over shrub was frequent. Several cheetahs chewed at leaves between sessions of cheek-rubbing the plants. Some of these plants were known to have been marked in the past but none were marked just before, during, or after the catnip response.

Unlike lions, cheetahs are not polyestrous. At Lion Country Safari mating activity was much more frequent during July, August, and September. It tapered off and from December through March was not observed at all. Our cheetahs at World Wildlife Safari were also imported from South West Africa and they showed first signs of courtship in mid-June, which continued through July. Then a more intense season occured from mid-October thru mid-November, in general the same as San Diego's cheetahs (Herdman, 1972).

⑥ Aggressive Behavior

I left Kenya in 1967, and used my data on social organization and spacing in cheetahs for a Master's Thesis at Purdue University. From 1968 to 1971, I studied social behavior in lions for a Ph.D. at Purdue, but not in Africa. Instead, I chose to investigate the lion's social life under semi-natural conditions at Lion Country Safari. With two sites, in Florida and California, and a total of over 300 lions, I was able to observe a number of prides over a long period. Under these conditions experimental manipulations could be carried out that would have been impossible in the wild. For example, once the status relations in a pride were clearly established, I was able to introduce a foreign lion and study the process of social integration. Mating and fighting behavior were as natural as in the wild, only continuous observation of each pride was possible. I knew what took place in a pride every day and why changes in dominance or mating preferences came about.

My major objective was to describe aggressive behavior and what induced it, but during the lion study, Lion Country Safari imported 24 wild cheetahs from South West Africa. This gave me an excellent opportunity to study aggression in cheetahs and to compare it to lions.

In all of the African literature on wildlife only two observations of fighting between cheetahs have been reported. Stevenson-Hamilton (1947) in South Africa recorded the fights, both of which involved one male fighting another at a kill site. Both combats resulted in death for one of the combatants. In Africa I had witnessed only slight aggression between a mother, in heat, inspected by her nearly adult son. A simple slap of the face was all it amounted to. If cheetahs do fight, even rarely, I was most intrigued to discover what caused it. Also it would be interesting to be able to see how they fought compared with other predators.

The setting of 24 cheetahs, the world's largest collection, in a small area was the perfect experimental situation to study fighting behavior. Surely the crowding would result in competition and aggression.

I spent all day and many nights in the cheetah section for about three months just after the cheetahs arrived from Africa. Later I spent late afternoons and early evenings, after the tourists left and the cheetahs became more active, watching the cheetahs for six more months. The results were illuminating. Indeed, cheetahs are aggressive in a number of situations and their fighting behavior quite stereotyped and complex.

After the tourists left one evening in July, 1970, we threw out a whole carcass of a horse. All the cheetahs, though already fed to satiation on cut-up fresh horsemeat, ran to the carcass. Immediately there was fighting, hundreds of fights in a manner of minutes! Fur literally flew through the air and the vocalizations were so many and so loud that I had trouble believing my ears. This experiment was repeated many times with typical cheetah prey that died in the reserve, for example gazelles, moufflon sheep, etc. When I analyzed the film and tape-recordings, the nature of fighting behavior became more discernible.

As the cheetahs are gathered around a carcass, they are all quite nervous. They are attracted to the carcass but at the same time are inhibited by the presence of many other cheetahs crowded around the carcass. When one cheetah turns its head and sees another standing close by looking at it, the outcome is inevitable—there is a short fight (Fig. 6–1). One of the cheetahs swats the other on the head; however, swatting in cheetahs is unique among the big cats. This is related to the specialized anatomy of the cheetahs. All of its claws on the forepaw except one are dull. The cheetah's claws are only partially retractile, and they are used in running. The claws on the front of the paw are not sharp and could not be effectively used in fighting. However, there is a large, slightly curved claw on the side of the foot which is not used in running and which is very sharp. It is this claw, the dew claw, which is used in swatting with the forepaw. It makes the opponent's fur fly (Fig. 6–2).

The blow is directed to the head of the opponent, usually the forehead or cheek. The dew claw is dug into the fur and skin and then pulled loose from the hide. This is the most common form of physical aggression. It is rarely injurious, and then only superficially.

The fight consisting of a single forepaw swat usually results in the

Figure 6–1   Fighting over a single carcass at Lion Country Safari. Notice that the animal swatting has its eyes closed. (Photo: R. L. Eaton.)

swatted cheetah actively submitting by rolling onto its side. Expression of submission usually "cuts off" or inhibits further attack. The submitter also emits high-pitched yelps, one after the other, once lying on its side, or when stared at prior to a potential attack.

Sometimes, around a carcass, there is a domino effect. A cheetah that submits by rolling onto its side away from the opponent, unknowingly makes contact with a third cheetah. The third cheetah then either attacks the submitter or in turn also submits and elicits attack or submission in a fourth cheetah. In this way fighting and submission move in a circle, from cheetah to cheetah, around the carcass.

Mere visual contact is enough to act as a threat and induce submission without there being any physical contact. In fact cheetahs actively avoid looking other cheetahs in the face. When crowded together at a carcass, it seems that every cheetah except those feeding is looking in a different direction. When one cheetah's eyes meet anothers, there is either a fight, one immediately submits, or both "look away," which itself is a form of submission.

The eyes have it, no doubt, and not just in the cheetah but also in

Figure 6–2 Visible here is the dewpaw, highly cornified and pointed. It is different from the dew claw hidden from view by hair. The dew claw is used both in fighting and predation. The paw is used only in fighting. (Photo: R. L. Eaton.)

wolves, lions and many primates, including man. A direct stare is a threat; looking away is submissive. There is one time when the eyes are always completely closed. That is during physical combat. Two fighters seal their eyes shut as soon as they initiate a swatting movement or are about to be struck. The dew claw could easily damage an eye, especially since it so often strikes the forehead. I believe that closure of the eyes is an adaptation that prevents eye injury.

The aggressive behavior at carcasses is not to be considered unnatural. Obviously the competing cheetahs possessed the ability to threaten, fight, and submit repeatedly in a predictable and stereotyped fashion. The absence of observing these behaviors in the wild is also explainable. At a carcass in the wild, there are rarely more than five or six cheetahs. Usually there is ample room for all the cheetahs to lie around the carcass and feed together. Furthermore, in the wild, the individuals that feed on the same carcass know each other well and probably already recognize and respond to an existing and stable dominance order.

In a situation with far too many cheetahs to feed simultaneously, plus the lack of long-term social relationships among individuals, increased competition and fighting should be expected.

There are many other expressions of aggression in cheetahs which also became known at Lion Country Safari. During the normal feeding procedure of throwing out whole chickens or cut-up horse or beef, there was competition. As one cheetah is lying down alone feeding, another approaches. If the possessor of the food looks up at the competitor or growls, the competitor quickly looks away as if not interested in the meat. As the competing cheetah gets closer and is again threatened with a stare or growl, he quickly turns around 180 degrees and faces directly away from the feeding cat. This wheeling around is repeated until the competitor's rear end is inches from the food and head of the feeding cheetah. The competitor remains sitting and occasionally glances over his shoulder at the food, eventually turning very quickly and grabbing the meat in his mouth. Sometimes this technique results in freeing the meat and making off with it. The presenting of the rear end as a means of approach to a potentially aggressive cheetah works because it removes the head and eyes from contact with the other cheetah. An animal that has its entire body facing completely away is obviously no real threat or danger. "I am not a competitor, how could I be in this orientation?," seems to be the information communicated. Presenting of the rear end in many primates plays a comparable role: it changes or redirects an attacker's motivation from aggression to sex.

Other times the original possessor has a good grip on the meat with his dew claws and teeth. There is a tug of war, which may last 15 minutes before one cheetah gives up or loses its grip.

The interesting thing about direct competition for food is that a rule emerges: "Possession is nine-tenths of the law." Once both cheetahs have a grip on the meat, neither swats the other though both are perfectly vulnerable. The goal is to obtain sole possession of the meat by maintaining a hold on it, and not to physically attack the other competitor and make him yield. This same rule holds true most of the time in lions also. Like cheetahs, lions with food are seldom physically attacked. Usually they are charged and threatened. The response is either to abandon the meat, for example to a more dominant lion, or to grip the meat in the claws and teeth so that the challenger cannot get it away. The cheetah or lion that lies there tightly holding the meat is extremely vulnerable to damaging attack, but the challenger is inhibited; he obeys the rules that have evolved to prevent harmful and possibly lethal damage.

The inhibitions which normally prevent lethal aggression favor the possessor. The result of leaving the food to threaten, fight, or chase a potential competitor away is usually futile as I have seen in both lions and cheetahs. Once the meat is abandoned, a third party quickly grabs it and runs away to feed, thus leaving the original competitors empty handed.

Very rarely a stereotyped form of physical attack is seen in cheetahs. It employs the use of another, unique anatomical specialty of the cheetah—the dew paws. All cats have fleshy dew paws on the back of their foreleg and above the pads on which the cat walks. However, the cheetah's dew paws, on each foreleg, are hard, pointed and sharp. The dew paws are not used in a head-on attack. Both paws are simultaneously raised up and brought down hard against another cheetah's shoulder or flank. They sometimes pierce the skin, inflicting puncture wounds.

Cheetahs are less formidable than lion, hyena, and leopard. The cheetah is slight in build, weighing less but taller and longer than a leopard. The cheetah's skull and jaws are reduced in size as a specialization for increased speed. Their claws are not especially dangerous either. Basically, they are ill-equipped to defend prey against competitors. In a few cases in Tanzania, cheetahs threatened approaching competitors, but in only one case did they succeed in preventing loss of their own kill, and that was against a single hyena. In all other instances, against several hyenas or a

Figure 6–3   Interspecific threat expression. (Photo: R. L. Eaton.)

lion, the cheetahs abandoned their kill. The threats were not backed up by physical contact. Descriptions of interspecific threatening have been incomplete and never captured on film. At Lion Country Safari I had a good chance to make many observations of the aggressive responses reserved for other species.

The mouth is opened wider in interspecific threat. The "open mouth" threat is a display of the teeth which is enhanced by the striking contrast of black gums and lips (Fig. 6–3). The wrinkles in the face, so typical of tiger, lion, and leopard, are seen in the cheetah in threatening lion, leopard, hyena, and man. The wrinkles in the face are seen in lion against lion, in leopard against leopard, and, so on, however, lion and leopard use the same expressions to communicate visually a threat or a warning to their own and other species alike. The cheetah is different in this respect, it mimics the competing predator's general threat expressions. For example, hissing, growling, and similar sounds have a similar effect among a variety of species. The cheetah does not hiss or growl at other cheetahs, but it does at other predators and men. This achieves what is in essence a common language. If a cheetah threatened a leopard the same way it did another cheetah, the leopard would not recognize and respond to the cheetah's expression. We find in the cheetah two different sets of behavioral patterns that express a warning and aggressive mood—one for their own species and another for other species.

The threatening between cheetahs is far more subtle and less exaggerated. A momentary stare and a slightly open mouth can easily elicit submission in another individual. Threatening against other species is far more intent but is never backed up with actual physical attack.

The first time I personally experienced an attack of a cheetah, I kept telling myself "cheetahs have never been known to attack people!" It was nearly dark as my wife and I walked through the cheetah section. Suddenly two cheetahs got up from 60 yards away and ran straight at us. I looked in horrified disbelief for a second, then stood in front of Katia, facing them, which often deters an animals attack (one has no chance if he runs!). The cheetahs kept on coming. When they were 20 feet away I thought to raise my windbreaker up over my head to arms length thus creating a huge silhouette against the dimly lit horizon. Both cheetahs suddenly came to a halt only five feet away. I still wonder if they did not perceive us as prey.

At a carcass at Lion Country, just as in the wild, cheetahs threaten man. Fritz Walther, the well-known ungulate ethologist, was once charged by cheetahs on a gazelle kill in the Serengeti. I studied under Walther and when he related the story to me it was quite a shock. This was the first report I had heard of a cheetah attacking man in the wild. Cheetahs had stalked me in the wild as I lay on the ground observing them. My standing

Figure 6–4 A Cheetahs threatening human with interspecific behavior not seen in aggression between cheetahs. (Photo: R. L. Eaton.)

up always ended their stalks and I was never attacked. The cheetahs had apparently perceived me as prey until I stood erect.

The cheetahs that charged Walther were responding to him exactly as they would to a hyena. Cheetahs attempt to defend kills against man and beast alike. Hundreds of times during feeding, I have been threatened by cheetahs as I walked nearby or purposely approached them (Fig. 6–4). The cheetah makes a short rush with its body angled slightly sideways so that the hind end is partially visible. The head is held low, the mane on the neck is raised, and an eerie moaning growl is emitted. The climax of this complex display is the "foot stamp." The cheetah lunges forward while raising both forelegs and then stamping them down on the ground. The stamp makes considerable noise and dust may fly. The foot stamp is accompanied by a sudden loud gush of air that creates a sound not unlike the "hai" of karate. The mouth is opened its widest during the foot stamp, throughout which the cheetah stares directly into your eyes. It is very frightening (Fig. 6–5).

The lowered head, the "moan," the "hai," the "foot stamp," and the prolonged stare have never been observed in hundreds of aggressive encounters between cheetahs. Truly, this complex of behavior is highly evolved and specialized for interactions with other species only. This is not a common thing among large cats, usually they warn or threaten their own and other species in the same way.

At World Wildlife Safari we avoid being near the cheetahs to prevent human contact and any undue stress which would conceivably interfere with breeding. However, periodic observation has revealed that our cheetahs also exhibit intra- and interspecific threat identical to that described above, though perhaps more intense since they see people and compete directly with other cheetahs far less than at Lion Country Safari.

Figure 6–4 B The author eliciting threat from cheetah. (Photo: K. Eaton.)

Figure 6–5 The foot stamp involves a forward lunge in which both forepaws strike the ground. (Photo: R. L. Eaton.)

7 *Predatory and Killing Behavior*

In 1965, the East Africa Wild Life Society conducted an investigation aimed at presenting all known aspects of cheetah life history (Graham and Parker, 1965). The answers to the question which asked for descriptions of cheetah kills consisted of 40 eye-witness accounts of cheetah making kills. Information from all observers resulted in the following conclusion: "The prey is knocked over, held down and killed, the actual cause of death being unknown." Denis (1964:39) described cheetah killing behavior as follows:

> Then comes the famous lightning dash ending with a blow at the victim's hind legs, or a spring at its throat or onto its back bringing hunter and hunted to the ground. Though neither teeth nor claws are as strong as a leopard's, they do not easily relax their grip, and death usually comes from a bitten jugular vein or windpipe.

The conclusion by Denis that death of the prey results from damage to the jugular vein or windpipe is held by other observers. Shortridge (1934:107) said, "Cheetah are said invariably to kill by strangulation, and seldom to relax their first grip on the throat until the animal is dead." Shortridge, like Denis, does not give any explicit data on how the throat is gripped, for example from what angle, or how it is damaged. Nor is there any detail on how the cheetah actually brings down the prey animal. Wendt (1959:57) said that cheetahs " . . . race after the prey, beat it down with their feet. . . ." Estes (1967:23) in writing about killing behavior says, "Leopards and lions, and particularly the cheetah also frequently kill large prey by gripping the throat until the animal suffocates." No exact information is given on how the animal is brought down or dispatched. Leyhausen (1965:452–453) describes killing behavior in the lion as composed of various steps including: seizing the animal from behind with both paws or one paw, and while biting and scratching the hind end, attempting to pull the animal down as it tries to escape. Once the animal is down it is held down and the bite is directed to the spinal area of the upper back or neck. Leyhausen concludes that death results from severing the spine. Schaller (1967:293) describes almost exactly the same behavioral sequence for tigers, only biting from the dorsal side of the neck in tigers is less common than gripping the throat from the ventral side. Schaller (1969) notes that lions kill most frequently by strangulation.

Leyhausen (1965) did not observe cheetah killing behavior but from extensive observations of various other *Felidae* concludes that the death of the prey is the result of damage from the teeth of the cat usually to the nervous system and that the fatal bite is at an angle from above or dorsal to the prey's neck. Schaller (1967:294) describes killing in tigers as consisting of two steps: ". . . (1) the attack, during which the animal is thrown off its feet, and (2) the actual killing, usually by biting into the throat or the back of the neck." Most of the time the death of prey is the result of the tiger holding the ventral side of the neck for several minutes until the animal suffocates. Schaller, however, did not examine tiger (or cheetah) kills to determine the area of damage from the ventrally directed killing bite. Leyhausen (pers. comm.) recently suggested that biting from the ventral side can also kill by damage to the central nervous system and that death in such cases may be quite prolonged.

This recent work on predatory behavior in the cat family with emphasis on killing behavior in the laboratory by Leyhausen (1956, 1965) and in the field, principally by Schaller (1968, 1969) can be verified here. I frequently observed predatory behavior in wild cheetahs. The cheetah does not typically exhibit the normal predatory behavior of the other cats; however, most of the cheetah's predatory sequence is essentially homologous to ". . . watching, crouching, stalking, seizing, and 'angling,' " as Leyhausen describes for many cats.

The cheetah watches prey intently, depending greatly on vision to determine at what time to stalk and attack. The cheetah watches for cues such as the attentiveness of the potential prey animals, for example alert calls and in which direction they are looking, and from this appears to be able to evaluate the general level of alertness or sense of danger in the prey.

The cheetah seldom crouches like most cats. Though Schaller (1972) interprets their stationary posture during hunting as crouching, I am using "crouching" as a descriptive not a functional term. It walks along slowly, looking for game, lifting the head up either to get a better view or to examine more closely game that has been spotted already. While the cheetah is close to prey it keeps its body low with its head higher than the body, rarely taking its eyes away from the game. The prey often notice movement or the silhouette of the cheetah. Before being recognized and responded to as a predator the cheetah in turn often recognizes that it is being watched, even if by only one animal in a large herd. The ability of the cheetah to recognize the slightest awareness of any of the herd enables it to stop and remain stationary until the prey lose interest. "Staring contests" of five to seven minutes between cheetah and small herds of prey are common at this stage of a hunt. The very instant that all of the prey appear not alert, the cheetah, without taking its eyes away from the prey, stalks a little further, again stopping instantly if an animal looks in its direction. The "crouch" aspect of predatory behavior in the cheetah is modified to a state of alertness that requires holding the head up high and remaining motionless enough to maintain visual contact with the prey. This visually oriented behavior enables the cheetah to approach the prey as close as possible before actually attacking.

"Pouncing" in most cats is homologous to the behavior in the cheetah that involves chasing and catching the intended prey animal. Most cats attack over very short distances and often the prey is not aware of the cat until it is very close or already upon the prey. Cheetah seldom make kills in this manner, but instead must bring down the prey while both are running very fast. In order to make a kill the cheetah must first overcome the prey and bring it down.

The cheetah knocks over the fleeing prey, the exact manner of which varies with the species of prey, its size, and how fast it is moving when overcome by the cheetah. For large prey species such as subadult kongoni I observed that the cheetah ran until it was along the flank of the animal. Then it struck with its forepaws posteriorally above the hind legs. Due to vegetation and dust it was not possible to see if the cheetah ever left contact with the ground completely. This blow knocked the animal over, and, as it fell, the cheetah quickly grabbed the throat on the ventral side with its mouth and exerted weight on the victim's anterior end by extending the front legs over the head and neck, one forelimb on each side of the neck hold. Schaller (1972) observed broken legs in gazelles which resulted from their being knocked down by cheetahs.

With smaller prey such as impala the cheetah knocked the prey over in the fashion described above. The grabbing and holding down of the prey once it is toppled is comparable to the "seizing" phase of the predatory sequence in house cats (Leyhausen, 1965).

With the young of large prey and very small game species or their young, such as warthogs, the cheetah simply lands on or hits the animal's body with one or both of its front legs as it runs up to and overcomes the animal from behind and above or from the side. When the animal falls over, usually rolling, the cheetah keeps the prey down by standing on it and/or then very quickly grabs the animal by the upper back or neck and carries or drags it to nearby cover where it is then killed and eaten. When the prey is dragged off, the cheetah grips it in the throat region. In open areas such as in parts of the Serengeti, the cheetah has little cover in which it can eat prey. Presumably cover hides the prey and the cheetah from potential scavengers or other predators. House cats also take captured prey to a secluded place where it is eaten; however, the prey is normally killed first (Leyhausen, 1956).

Cheetah spend several minutes killing prey. Five minutes is common but for some cheetahs 15–25 minutes was not rare, even with small impala fawns. Some prey revive from strangulation killing attempts and have to be "strangled" two to three more times before death occurs.

Prey such as young warthogs have very short and thick necks. They offer relatively little space for the cheetah to grip the throat. In these cases inflicting death appeared difficult. Death sometimes came from crushed skulls since the bones are soft in very young prey and the brain is easily damaged. A bite directed to the dorsal side of a young warthog's neck was observed, but death resulted from a crushed skull, not from spinal damage or blood loss.

Blood was seldom seen externally on the bodies of prey during or shortly following killing. In order to determine whether or not death was, in fact, the result of strangulation, the head and the neck of prey were examined immediately after the cheetah left the carcass. The head and upper neck are normally not consumed by cheetah except in very young animals that are eaten entirely. Teeth did not puncture major vessels and no necks were broken or damaged. Slight rupture and hemorrhaging in the ventral and lateral parts of the upper neck were common but the loss of blood was not appreciable, and apparently not the cause of death. Punctures of the prey's skin were slight and not always present. The trachea or larynx were not removed for examination to determine collapse or damage. However, death is probably not the result of injury to the nervous or circulatory systems. In all probability death is the result of strangulation. Dr. Fritz Walther (pers. comm.) has confirmed these observations with his own. He noted that gazelles killed by cheetah died of apparent strangulation, and Schaller (1968:99) says, on the basis of examining 136 carcasses believed to be cheetah kills, that "Gazelle are killed by strangulation. . . ."

ONTOGENY OF KILLING BEHAVIOR

One litter of four cheetah cubs and a parent adult female were observed closely from the time the cubs were about 5½ months old until they were 9½ months old. Fewer observations were made of two other litters aged 6–10 and 10–14 months during the field study.

Behavior suggestive of predatory instincts is observed in very young cheetah. Predatory related behavior in cubs only two weeks old was observed by Stevenson-Hamilton (1947). He states, ". . . when one of them rushed at a terrier which had gotten into the cage he struck at the dog with his forepaws as he charged, just as a domestic cat often does." It is possible that the cubs were exhibiting the predatory component that adults use to knock prey down. Encke (1960) says about captive cheetah cubs, "The typical cheetah-type attack (knocking the prey down with the paws) was first noticed at about the eleventh or twelfth week." Data on cheetah from the wild prior to hunting experience support a different hypothesis. Crandall (1964:396) says, "Just as wildcaught birds are preferred to hand-reared ones by the falconer, so is the cheetah with natural hunting experience esteemed by the trainer." Sterndale (1884:200) says, "For this purpose the adult animal is always caught, it being considered by the chita-catchers that a young leopard would never turn out well for the purposes of the chase." Shortridge (1934:108) said, "In Northern India and Persia, where they are sometimes trained to hunt blackbuck and chikara, it is said to be essential to capture adult animals for this purpose, since the cubs do not develop the required skill unless first taught by their parents." Denis (1964:68) said, ". . . it could catch Bennet's gazelles but not pull them down; it appears that the hunting leopard has to be taught by its parents. The speed but not the kill is inherited."

One female with cubs gave a low pitched "ughh" that had the effect of keeping the cubs in one place while she was gone. They remained still until she gave a high-pitched "chirp" which brought the cubs to kill site. When the cubs were about six months old the mother showed intense interest in an adult warthog with two newly born young and for the first time allowed the cubs to follow. The cheetah and the cubs slowly approached the warthogs, all of them exhibiting typical stalking behavior. The cubs had often watched their mother stalk but lacked experience with game themselves. The warthogs were "rooting" and facing away from the cheetahs. The cheetahs approached from 100 yards at about half speed until when about 30 yards away the warthogs began to run. The mother cheetah instantly exhibited full-speed chase but ran beyond the young warthogs and pursued the adult. The cubs proceeded to give chase after the young warthogs while the adult cheetah kept running back and forth between the adult warthog and the young warthogs. (When the adult warthog stays with the young warthogs even groups of adult cheetahs cannot prey upon the young successfully unless the young can be separated from the parent.) The adult warthog finally stopped "trying" to reach her young and the adult cheetah then ran back to follow her cubs while they chased one of the young warthogs. The cubs followed closely behind the warthog, within inches at times, but showed no movements indicative of an attempt to knock over or grab it. It appeared that the adult cheetah could have caught the prey at any time but instead ran closely behind the cubs. After three minutes of chasing, one warthog was out of sight and the one being chased ran into a hole.

In several similar hunts the cubs were allowed to chase the prey but the female caught it. The prey was not dispatched but appeared to be in a state of shock and remained down while the cubs bit the animal in several places (but not the anterior end). Similar observations were made by Schaller (1972) and others in the Serengeti.

Another litter of four cubs at about 12 months of age could catch and kill typical prey. The actual learning of how to kill was not observed but it can be inferred that for cheetah cubs to bring down and kill prey, experience between the ages of 9 and 12 months is necessary, though Schaller (1972) states that cubs may capture prey by themselves by the age of about 8–12 months. The observations of the younger litter can surely be considered lessons in hunting. The instinctive behavior of stalking and chasing prey are manifest at a very young age in play. They apparently require little or no experience as compared with killing. The cubs may have to learn the stimuli (prey) to which they direct the "knocking-over" behavior pattern which apparently is innate. During play, cubs bite one another on the neck from the dorsal side and this implies an innate orientation for biting that is altered by experience to the ventral bite in killing prey. However, in early morning mock fights in adult cheetahs, biting was directed dorsally to the neck implying that the dorsal bite is not just a phylogenetic remnant and may function in intraspecific behavior, for example in mating or serious fighting, and it was observed in mating at Lion Country Safari. The cubs observe the female stalking and chasing prey for several months before they hunt with her. Learning by observations may be going on but in the field this was not possible to determine. The effect of experience on innate stalking behavior is pointed out by the observations of Kruuk and Turner (1967) in the Serengeti, where adult cheetah rarely stalk, but the cubs exhibit stalking frequently. However,

Schaller (1968) observed a female with cubs in the Serengeti that stalked often.

The adult cheetah is probably a requisite for the cubs to learn to catch and kill prey. Whether observational learning occurs in the cubs or simply the opportunity to practice, develop, and improve innate behavior patterns is not known. Stevenson-Hamilton (1947:199–200) said of two cubs raised by a ranger, ". . . they took to absenting themselves in the evenings for gradually prolonged periods, until at last they failed to return and were seen no more." Speculation would lead to the belief that the cubs were able to catch animals, perhaps crippled or vulnerable prey, and learned to kill properly after a few attempts. They were being fed by men; otherwise they probably would have starved before the predatory sequence was perfected.

FURTHER STUDIES

My field study provided details of the hunting behavior (Eaton, 1970a) and predatory sequence (Eaton, 1970b) of the cheetah in the wild. Since these findings were reported I have been able to study experimentally and observe repeatedly predatory and feeding behavior under improved observational conditions in seminatural conditions. I have discovered much additional information and even changed some earlier conclusions derived from study in the wild.

The cheetahs I observed were kept adjacent to an ungulate area which included gazelles, zebra, waterbuck, lechwe, sitatunga, rhinoceros, giraffe, addax, elephant, and hippopotamus. Only a fence separated the ungulates from the cheetahs, which had a clear view of the ungulates and vice-versa.

Even when fed to the point of fully distended stomachs and with much fresh meat still available, cheetahs responded to dead, whole chickens, white in color. They exhibited a form of predatory play behavior which consisted of raising the front end up off the ground then coming down with both forefeet striking the chicken, much as coyotes and foxes do when catching mice. When fed the larger, whole carcasses of horse, gazelle, moufflon sheep, etc., these responses were not seen.

The striking with both or one foreleg is not seen elsewhere in predatory behavior though I earlier believed that the dew paw was employed in striking the fleeing prey and that this physical blow knocked the prey over; however, this is not the case. The use of one or both dew paws is restricted to play with prey and conspecifics and to fighting.

On several occasions an abundance of cut-up horsemeat was fed until the cheetahs stopped feeding. After reaching what was considered satiation, a whole carcass of a horse or other ungulate was introduced.

Figure 7–1 Captive cheetahs, satiated on prepared meat, feed ravenously when a whole carcass is presented. (Photo: R. L. Eaton.)

Immediately the cheetahs fed ravenously, and did not stop until all was consumed, except for the skin, larger bones, skull, stomach, and intestines (Fig. 7–1).

In some carcass feedings, there were cheetahs that delivered the killing bite to the upper, ventral throat of the carcass, exactly as is seen in the wild and by these same cheetahs to live prey.

Carcasses were dragged behind a vehicle into the cheetah area. The cheetahs immediately ran to and chased the carcass, some of them digging the dew claw into the carcass and pulling backwards as it moved forward.

Models in the form of mounted specimens were brought into the cheetah area to test the responses of the cheetahs. A mounted specimen of a gazelle was placed on the ground 50 yards from the closest cheetahs, all of which were lying down. The first cheetahs to approach walked slowly to the model. Olfactory inspection continued for several minutes, primarily at the anterior and posterior ends of the model. Other cheetahs that eventually saw the cheetahs inspecting the model ran to the model. Those that ran from a direction that brought them directly in front of and facing the model's head stopped abruptly and threatened the model's head before walking around to the side and then olfactorily inspecting the model (Figs. 7–2 and 7–3).

After about ten minutes, one female attacked the model by raising up in the front, her weight shifted posteriorally as she reached both forelegs out and over the back of the model, bringing both forepaws down on the model, digging the dew claws into the model and pulling it towards her.

These experiments were repeated several times and after the first trial, with one of two gazelle models, the model became surrounded by as many cheetahs that could lie around it side by side, usually about six. One or two of the same females always "killed" the gazelle by biting it on the ventral throat and holding this, the suffocation bite. The other cheetahs tried to eat the model, biting into it and trying to tear the hide, until they were driven away.

The cheetahs employed the interspecific threat behavior when we approached and took the model away. These threats, reserved for the interspecific realm, are seen in the wild when cheetahs are approached by competing predators. They are never followed by a physical attack, neither are they ever seen in intraspecific threat or fighting.

Figure 7–2 Cheetahs investigating a mounted gazelle specimen. (Photo: R. L. Eaton.)

Figure 7–3 Cheetah exhibits some fear and inhibition while facing gazelle specimen. (Photo: R. L. Eaton.)

Prior to any experiments in which live prey were released into the cheetah's area, observations of the response of cheetah to live prey in the adjacent area were made. Would formerly wild-living cheetahs, kept well fed, go on "hunting" prey that was visually accessible, and at times only inches away separated only by a fence?

Indeed, the cheetahs' response to live prey that they could not catch, kill, or eat (that is, their behavior was not reinforced) maintained a high level of expression over one year's period, beginning six months after they had been removed from the wild and any contact with live prey. The onset of live feeding during this period did not alter the level of their hunting behavior of the inaccessible prey.

The cheetahs stalked and observed prey in a number of postures typical of wild, hunting cheetahs. They often lay close to the fence separating them from distant prey and also sought higher-elevation areas from which they intently watched far distant prey and wild native deer and livestock, outside the reserve confines, as distant as 1000 yards or more. Prey that was closer or approached the cheetah area were actively hunted. In several cases, typical prey species walked right to and along the separation fence. The cheetahs then attacked the prey at the fence, sometimes starting the prey to running along the fence in which case the cheetahs ran alongside the running prey. Many times a prey at the fence or up to 200 yards distant turned and ran away. This immediately released a chasing attack in most of the cheetahs. There was no doubt that, as found in the wild, running away releases predatory attack.

Of special interest was the cheetah's response when standing and facing prey inches away on the other side of the fence (equally noteworthy is the fact that some captive-born prey species hunted by cheetahs in the wild showed little or no fear when charged by cheetahs). The cheetahs responded variously, including threatening the prey, swatting the fence, and, most curious, running away a few yards, turning around and charging the prey. It was as if the cheetahs were trying to make the prey run away (as though this would enhance success of an obviously impossible hunt). It also resulted in frequent short fight encounters between those cheetahs closest to the prey at the fence, when they looked around and saw other cheetahs close by and apparently staring at them, a threat.

It should be mentioned that the cheetahs that showed least interest in prey were the few subadults. They had been captured in the wild at ages of five to seven months of age, just as their "education" in hunting and prey-killing would have begun. Apparently the lack of hunting education and experience affected their motivation to "hunt" the visually but not physically available prey. Experiments with a naive cheetah, imported into the United States at five months of age, showed that typical killing was elicited by live prey after three trials in which an experienced cheetah killed as the naive cheetah observed and then fed. Such a complex behavior could not be learned by imitation, but rather seemed to be evoked by excitation from observation and feeding.

Hunting of the inaccessible prey was not less intense following normal feeding, but was decidedly less so after feeding from carcasses, when greatly more food is consumed. Hunting activity was highest, regardless of proximity of prey, in the early and late daylight hours as well as on bright moonlight evenings. This has been well established for wild cheetahs.

Only a few adults killed live chickens, though nearly all cheetahs chased and caught them. The chickens were white, unlike any likely prey encountered in South West Africa. I am told by Bill York that when he fed black chickens to captive, wild-caught cheetahs in Africa, they always killed and ate them, as they do the more darkly colored guinea fowl in Africa.

Chickens that "froze" were softly pawed repeatedly. Those that ran were chased. Two cheetahs killed all of the two dozen chickens, and they did so with bites to the upper neck and head which they held for up to several minutes, typical of the suffocating bite used on mammalian prey.

A few of the cheetahs plucked and ate the chickens while most of them

Figure 7–4 Cheetahs chase, bring down and kill fleeing goats. Note the rudder-like use of the tail as cheetah changes directions (lower right). (Photo: R. L. Eaton.)

ignored the chickens once they were dead. Fowl is not a significant prey item in the wild, and excluding color, possibly as an imprinted stimulus, there is a very good chance that most of these cheetahs never killed or ate fowl of any kind previously. However, all the cheetahs did feed on an adult ostrich carcass, which is far larger, has been recorded more often as prey than smaller fowl, and which is sparsely covered with feathers.

A number of live prey, moufflon sheep and goats—mammals of the same size as typical cheetah prey—were introduced into the cheetah area. All of the cheetahs attacked and chased these prey; however, it was the adults that always killed them with the suffocation bite. Surprisingly enough, as many as 12 cheetahs sometimes had difficulty in bringing down one sheep or goat. This was the result of the fact that the prey were so close. When they ran the prey were moving so slowly that they could not easily be knocked off balance. Also, the cheetahs' speed was slow, preventing them for using the movements normally effective at greater speeds.

When the prey was released further away and/or ran faster away from the cheetahs, there was no difficulty in bringing the fleeing prey down and quickly dispatching it (Fig. 7–4).

In filming these interactions with live prey, which I was unable to do in the wild, I discovered additional aspects of predatory behavior which went unnoticed and undescribed in my earlier field work. As it turns out, finer analysis proves that the cheetah's predatory sequence fits more closely the behavior of other felids than previously believed.

For example, as Fig. 7–4 depicts, the fleeting prey is not knocked over with a blow from the cheetah's forepaw(s). In fact, the dew claw is most critical in the component functionally labeled "bringing prey down." The claw is inserted in the prey's hide and the cheetah's weight is shifted posteriorally (Fig. 7–4) thus exerting a posterior force on one side of the forward moving prey. This causes the prey to lose balance; its rear legs fold under and it falls to its side.

Also worth emphasizing is the use of the tail in making fast changes of direction, as shown in Fig. 7–4.

It is even more remarkable that at great speeds, accurately measured to be as high as 71 miles per hour, the cheetah is able in one motor sequence, to momentarily shift its weight posteriorally while extending the forepaw to bring down the prey(Fig. 7–4).

With slower-running prey cheetahs grab ahold with both dew claws on the fleeing prey's hind end, shift their weight backwards, and pull back with the forepaws, thus weighting and bringing the prey down.

These observations also established that the orientation of the killing bite is elicited in a more elaborate manner. Once the prey is fallen the cheetah approaches the head from the dorsal side of the lying prey. The head and upper neck are rotated towards the cheetah by digging one dew claw into the head or upper neck and pulling, while holding the prey down with the other foreleg placed over the lying prey's shoulders and lower neck, which prevents the entire body from rolling as the head and neck are rotated (Fig. 7–5).

During these movements the cheetah lowers its head so that the mouth faces posteriorally. The upper ventral neck of the prey is gripped in the mouth. Once the neck grip is achieved, the cheetah uses this grip to rotate the neck (and head) towards itself, thus twisting the neck. When the ventral neck is rotated laterally the cheetah holds the bite and suffocates the prey.

This complex of orientations and movements accomplishes at least two things. It prevents the cheetah from being exposed to the hooves of the fallen prey, and by rotating the neck and head upwards, the horns are moved further away. Perhaps the twisting of the neck also makes the trachea more vulnerable to collapse from the throat bite. Examination of three gazelle carcasses, killed by cheetah from South West Africa, showed two with collapse of the trachea and one whose spine was crushed.

At greater distances the twisting technique was not observed in East African cheetahs, but was observed in cheetahs from South West Africa. Perhaps, as Eloff (1973) has found in the Kalahari lion, a specialized killing

Figure 7–5 Experienced in the wild, this captive cheetah quickly kills a sheep. The head is rotated while the throat is gripped thus suffocating the prey.

technique is culturally evolving in the cheetahs of South West Africa. This hypothesis is unlikely since cheetah cubs could learn only from their own mother, and it is adult groups of males that show the highest specializations in predatory behavior.

There are several possible reasons why some of the larger cats kill by strangulation as opposed to biting at the nape of the neck and inflicting central nervous system damage as occurs in smaller cats. Leyhausen (1965:488) points out that biting is specialized in the cats for killing and the forelimbs for seizing. This certainly is the case for tigers, cheetahs, lions, and perhaps for the leopard. Leyhausen states further,

> This evolutionary process is paralleled by the development of the canine teeth, which, by their structure, shape and position in the jaws, have become well adapted to being wedged between the vertebrae of a prey animal's neck. The vertebrae are thus disconnected and the hind brain or spinal cord is lacerated, which results in instantaneous death. Feline canine teeth are quite unsuitable for crunching hard bones or piercing large blood vessels.

Lions use the teeth behind the canine for crushing bones when feeding at a kill and this supports Leyhausen's view that canines are not adapted for crushing. D. Simpson (pers. comm.) relates that adult male lions kill two year old lions by crushing their skulls with the canines. Leopards may kill some of the time by using their canines to crush skulls, for example of primates and the young of many species.

The cheetah's canines in fact have not been specialized at all for piercing the spine of prey. The cheetah is comparable in weight with the leopard, both ranging between about 100 and 150 pounds. The skull measurements are vastly different than in the leopard, which has much larger skull and teeth measurements (Roberts, 1951:564–565). The leopard is more typical of other cat species in skull and tooth size and proportions. It is also more typical in the way it hunts, employing pouncing from trees or stalking and pouncing from distances very close to the prey. It is to be expected that the canines would be selected to be relatively large since killing as opposed to stalking and pouncing make up a more important part of the overall predatory sequence in the leopard as compared with the cheetah.

The method of capturing prey in the leopard has probably led to selection for the larger skull and teeth which are used to kill by severing and crushing parts of the neck and skull, as well as for strangulation. Besides longer canines, the leopard's carnassials have cusps on the inner edges which are an adaptation for crushing; the cheetah lacks these cusps.

Acting on cheetah killing behavior are opposing selection forces: selection for speed which favors reduced skull and teeth size, and counteracting selection pressure on skull and tooth size large enough to dispatch prey effectively. Rapid death of captured prey is especially important to prevent disabled, but live animals, from vocalizing and attracting other predators and scavengers. Graham and Parker (1965) noted that in many cases, cheetah have been driven from their kills by lions, leopards, and hyenas, and even jackals. Pienaar (1969) and Schaller (1968) also noted the frequent robbing of cheetahs' kills by other predators in Kruger Park, South Africa, and the Serengeti Area, respectively.

Strangulation appears to be a behavioral adaptation that counteracts the would-be anatomical deficiencies that are modifications for speed. Without strangling behavior the cheetah would be anatomically unequipped for killing many prey. Leyhausen (pers. comm.) noted that the lack of the diastema (the space between the canine and the molars) in the cheetah's jaw supports the conclusion that cheetah are unable to use the canine to pierce the prey's spine (however, this does occur with small antelope).

The cheetah's mouth is so small that it usually must bite and strangle from the ventral side of the prey's throat; however, probably in the cheetah, and certainly in other species, another factor favors such an orientation—the danger to the predator from the horns or antlers of the prey. The cheetah holds the prey down with both forelegs and its mouth. Twisting the head so that the horns point to the ground, lies at right angles to the prey and close to its head, which gets it far away from the legs and horns of the prey.

There appear to be other ways for lions to avoid injury from their captured prey. Eloff (1964, 1973) describes cases in the Kalahari region, South Africa, of gemsbocks goring with their horns and killing attacking lions. Eloff suggests that the Kalahari lions have adaptively modified their predatory behavior by breaking the prey's back before proceeding to kill the disabled prey with a ventral strangle hold or dorsal neck bite. The lions attack in one of their usual ways from behind, but once the lion is on top of the haunches it grips the posterior dorsal surface in its teeth and pulls upward, thereby breaking the back between the last lumbar and first sacral vertebra and snapping the spinal cord (kills were dissected to determine the nature of these injuries). This vertebral region is especially weak to upward but not downward force.

PREDATION COMPARED TO AGGRESSION

How is aggression related to predation? Is the motivation in fighting the same as the drive to kill a prey animal? It is widely accepted that aggression in large predators is inhibited so as to prevent death and injury to members of the species. If lions fought each other in the same way they effectively kill buffalo, they would soon kill themselves off. I studied the expressions and behavior of cheetah in hunting and killing prey to see how these compared to their threat and fight behavior between themselves.

When cheetahs stalk, attack, and chase prey they show no overt signs of aggression. The mouth is usually closed, the eyes are fixed on the prey, and there is no growling or vocalization of any kind. The prey is not swatted. Instead it is knocked off balance with the backward pull resulting from the dew claw dug into the flanks of the prey. Without the single dew claw on the forepaw, a cheetah could not bring down the majority of its prey. The teeth are used only to kill the prey.

The cheetah only rarely employs its teeth in fighting. There is a ritualized or inhibited bite directed to the cheek, but it is short in duration and not damaging. It acts more as a threat that communicates: "Go away or I might do you real harm." In the most severe fights there are bites delivered to the forelegs primarily, but never to the throat. In summary it can be concluded that the use of the prey-killing tools—teeth and claws—does not resemble the use of these same tools in fighting.

One of the most surprising results of predator—prey behavioral interactions is that cheetahs do threaten prey. This occurs only rarely, in the unusual circumstance of the prey that does not take flight. Cheetahs are so specialized for catching swift prey on the run that they are helpless when an ungulate stands its ground. To kill the prey it must first be brought down to the ground, and this is possible only when the prey runs away. It is the forward movement of the prey coupled with the opposing pull of the cheetah's forepaw that causes the prey to fall.

Cheetahs respond to a prey that stands and faces them by exhibiting the complex of interspecific threats. They lunge and foot stamp, growl and show their teeth. Sometimes this response puts the prey to flight and it is then overcome and killed. Other times the prey is successful in avoiding death by refusing to flee or by even making short charges at the cheetahs and driving them away.

The cheetah is no exception to other predators that have so far been studied, in that actual physical aggression is limited and rarely damaging. Also, like other predators, the cheetah exhibits aggressive behavior that is different from its predatory behavior. Unlike many other predators, the cheetah is often a prey animal, due to its many adaptations for speed. Because it is anatomically ill-equipped to defend its kills, a compensating set of interspecific threat gestures has evolved, which mimic the threats of the cheetah's competitors. The precise way in which the forepaws are used in fighting is different from other cats due, again, to an anatomy in this case, the feet and claws, that is modified for speed.

8 Management and Behavior of Wild Cheetahs in Captivity

I have expressed my views on the ability of many American zoos in keeping and breeding endangered species. Even the best zoos often have a higher mortality than birth rate. This is abominable and inexcusable, especially regarding rare and endangered species. During visits and lectures at the best American zoos, the number of species on display, sometimes several thousand, were proudly pointed out to me. It is usually the case in the zoo world that quality is measured by number of species.

This approach is wrong. The goal should be to improve the quality of displays for a few species. No zoo is qualified to properly design displays for so many species. Nor can any particular zoo expect to keep thousands of species in artificial habitats that attempt to duplicate each species' natural setting. Instead, one zoo should specialize in a few groups of animals, say carnivores, large African mammals, or aquatic birds. Each zoo could then establish the protocols for improved keeping and breeding of its animals.

An animal in a barren cage with a plaque listing the animal's scientific name, range, and food habits is meaningless to the great majority of zoo tourists. I am optimistically convinced that hamsters, bull-snakes, and house cats, properly displayed, could prove more educational and interesting than thousands of labeled cages, one after the other. Zoos should rely on their animals' behavior to entertain and inform the public. We have museums that display the wonder of diversity that exists in nature. Zoos should be where the behavior of animals is observed, but behavior requires space, and often several individuals of the same species.

Some zoos are now expanding their displays, including several species in one area, for example wolves and bears. Others are developing wild animal parks which are modeled after Lion Country Safari. The emergence of the private-enterprise wildlife park has stimulated this new movement in the zoo world, and will lead to improvements for the researcher, the animal, and the tourist. Of particular value is the increased amount of space available to large mammals in the animal park. While cheetahs have bred recently in conventional zoos, for example Whipsnade, England; Prague, Czechoslovakia; and Toledo, Ohio, I believe that these births are exceptional, owing to particularly tolerant individuals, and recent arrival as adults from the wild state. What is needed is the best way to predictably breed the majority of captive cheetahs. The wild animal parks should establish these protocols, and are making progress toward this end.

In the cheetah, space is critically important to allow courtship and mating, and at Lion Country Safari courtship behavior was readily observed. Also significant to breeding success is the information gathered on managing wild cheetahs in seminatural conditions. (Eaton and Craig, 1973a).

It must be realized that the environment of the wildlife park established for tourist visitation is unique. The problems of successfully managing exotic species are qualitatively different from those in the zoological garden. The fact that Lion Country Safari had the world's largest collection of cheetahs made it a desirable research site to assist in laying the groundwork for large-scale breeding programs. At World Wildlife Safari we have established a breeding area for our cheetahs which is outside the drive-through reserve. If we succeed in breeding them, we might display them to visitors, but otherwise will not. Lion Country Safari has removed several of their cheetahs to a remote hillside for breeding purposes (Fig. 8–11), a decided improvement; however, behavioral disruption resulting from previous crowding might prove to be irreversible.

At Lion Country Safari most of the cheetahs appeared to adapt within a period of two weeks to the new area and to customer traffic. Since it was necessary to provide an attractive display to the public a certain amount of conditioning was necessary. This was accomplished by: (1) driving cheetahs out of areas where they were not easily visible from the road; (2) placement of shade trees near the road; and (3) feeding only in certain areas. For the most part the cheetah appeared to be oblivious to customer traffic. Since there was always a sufficient number of cheetahs on display, those individuals that did not respond well to training methods were not continually harassed.

Figure 8–1 Bill York of Lion Country Safari releases cheetahs from South West Africa. (Photo: B. Koch.)

After two months the cheetahs became so accustomed to traffic that they followed individual cars through the section in order to lie in their shade. In many instances cheetah were lying partially under the car. Contrary to expectation, most cheetahs responded neutrally to a high frequency of low-flying jet aircraft. At all times during visiting hours it was possible to maintain a display of at least two-thirds of the cats within 30 ft of the road. I should note here that while cars and aircraft appeared not to disturb cheetahs, appearances are deceiving. In live-trapping red and gray foxes in South Carolina, red foxes exhibited many signs of stress and threatened frequently. On the other hand, gray foxes appeared quite relaxed and were virtually placid. Once released in a captive area and observed from a great distance, both species exhibited high levels of activity in looking for an escape route. I became convinced that we too often expect overt behavior to reflect internal moods.

At first sight the Lion Country Safari cheetahs appeared to be one large, socialized group which indeed they were—all cheetahs tolerated and were generally friendly to one another (except for the injured female). However, within this large group, definite social affinities existed. In one area of shade there were commonly the same 10–12 individuals. The other 12 made up one smaller group of three to five and one or two lone individuals that periodically associated with one or both of the two groups or lay up alone. During hot summer months the two groups were relatively stable and they lay up together throughout most of the day from 9:30 a.m. to 5:00 p.m. The larger group lay up under an olive tree 20 ft from the road. Most of the other cheetahs avoided traffic and lay up at a rockpile or in the moat surrounding the section. In early morning, cheetahs were usually seen at the higher elevations in the section either visually exploring outside or resting. Play fighting and chasing was frequent in the early hours but this was completely exhibited by two or more of the same four or five cheetahs. These same cheetahs elicited play stalking and charges toward the keeper during their play sessions.

In summer cheetahs retired to shade before mid-morning, at about the time of the first tourists' arrival. The larger group went to the olive tree. Certain individuals exhibited more amicable behavior-greeting and social grooming to all other cheetahs but at higher frequencies to the more responsive individuals. Following feeding amicable behavior was frequent but social preferences were less obvious.

In favored lying-up spots, activity was initiated by one cat rolling over or changing its position among a tightly clustered group. This often initiated grooming sessions. It also resulted in abbreviated spats between only two cats or spreading through the entire group until all cats were involved. Following this domino effect, most cats were sitting up before all lay down again. From the onset of the first cheetah's rolling over and initiating a series of aggressive encounters until return of peace usually 10–15 seconds passed. Occasionally, one or two individuals left the group and moved to nearby shade areas where they lay up alone or in smaller groups.

In the later afternoon, with temperatures dropping, cheetahs became more active. Marking, drinking, and movement throughout the section was accompanied by sitting or lying down while visually scanning the surrounding area and often fixing on antelope in the adjacent section. On a large log in a higher area in the compound, fully mature cheetahs often stood and visually scanned for as long as 20 minutes. While visually oriented to the area outside the section, several mature males sat on high areas and uttered a meow-like sound, to which no other cheetahs responded.

Shortly after arrival, during the summer months there was considerable courting behavior. One female was actively courted until late November, while no other females courted after August. Behavioral estrus lasted two weeks on the average and there was usually a two week inter-estrous period. In August and September, the one female exhibited behavioral estrus for five consecutive weeks; and she was given a hormone shot (Stilbesterol: 75 mg) on October 16, 1970. After the hormone administration there was no increase in ongoing courtship behavior. She was seen mated on three occasions, July 21 and 31 at 7:30 P.M. and 8:30 P.M.; and October 1, at mid-day. The mated female was isolated on December 20, 1970, in case she was pregnant, although a mating was not observed in December. Later she died from an apparent liver ailment, the only mortality in the group.

As winter set in, many of the cheetahs were found together in one large group lying on the straw in the hut, or occasionally lying on the straw in one or more small groups outside the hut. The entire huddle of 20 or more cheetahs exhibited social affinities in that certain pairs or small groups preferred lying next to each other. For example, the two largest and apparently oldest males were usually together. They were nearly identical in appearance and I believe them to be brothers. The two males followed each other and fed together, did not compete for food, and were often seen lying together away from the group. The group of five (1:4) cheetahs that so often exhibited play were nearly always together when the hut was inspected in early morning. These five looked very much alike and appeared to be at the same age at arrival. There is little doubt that these associations reflect social groups from the wild.

FEEDING AND BEHAVIOR

The diet was varied little throughout the study. The staple ration was cut up, freshly slaughtered horsemeat, totaling about 4 pounds per day, 5 days a week. The amount fed was altered according to the cheetahs' appearance—whether thin or heavy. Water consumption was extremely low. Tidbiting amounted to a small portion of food but was used to manipulate the location of cheetahs to enhance the display. During the nine-months study period, cheetahs were fed a number of live prey and whole carcasses including: 15 goats, 7 moufflon sheep, 1 horse, 2 camels, 2 giraffe, 1 black buck, 1 ostrich, and many chickens and rabbits (Fig. 7–1). Aggressive behavior was intense when carcasses were fed since there wasn't enough space for all cheetahs to feed at one time. Of all the carcasses only the second camel was not entirely consumed. After the first camel was eaten, there were many piles of vomit on the following morning. Both camels weighed about 800 pounds and it was thought that perhaps overeating was the cause of vomiting; however, vomiting was also common after the second camel was fed although less than half of it was eaten. Furthermore, on a later date five moufflon sheep and one giraffe totaling at least 1200 pounds were fed at the same time and all but the large bones, skin, and stomach contents were consumed. Using 60% of carcass weight, the average amount eaten by each cheetah was nearly 30 pounds over a ten-hour period. The next morning every cheetah's belly was highly distended. They showed no activity and did not vomit. Chickens and rabbits were fed periodically and used as a medium for transfer of worming medicine. A specially prepared vitamin-mineral powder supplemented the meat diet.

Initially, a pickup truck with a specially caged-in bed was used to feed. The cheetahs soon became conditioned and ran toward the truck as it approached the section. Once in the section the truck stopped and individual pieces of meat were thrown out after being dipped in the powder supplement. Extra pieces for any supplementary feeding were left with the warden. Transferring the meat from truck to warden involved the warden leaving his jeep and passing near feeding cheetahs. Two medium-sized mature males commonly charged the warden; they dropped their meat and approached in the typical threat posture—head down, shoulders up, mouth open, tail curled under the stomach—accompanied by the moaning and spitting vocalizations and the foot stamping at the termination of the charge 10–20 ft from the warden (Fig. 6–5). After several months one of these same males charged closer, stopping only three or four feet away; physical contact was not made. Flight was readily induced by rushing at the threatening cheetah. Eye-to-eye contact with a cheetah induced threat, and when prolonged, resulted in flight and the avoidance of the human.

Feeding pieces of meat to all the cheetahs at one time did not reflect dominance. However, it was difficult to keep track of individuals and the outcome of competitive encounters. Typically the cheetah grabbed a piece of meat and ran away 30–50 meters before lying down to eat. Tugs of war occurred when two cats grabbed the same piece of meat and ran with it across the section, both gripping the meat in their mouth. The contests lasted as long as 10 minutes before one cat gave up or the meat was torn into two pieces. Consumption of a four-pound piece of meat normally required one to two minutes or less. Cheetahs with bony pieces first ate the meat then chewed on the bones for 5–15 minutes; those with pure meat were soon up, walking around, inspecting the ground for more, or approaching a feeding cheetah.

The approach consisted of trotting or walking to the feeding cat and when only three or four feet away, wheeling around with the rear end close to the feeding animal's head. The "presenter" then moved slowly backwards until his rear end was only inches from the other's head, and finally turned and attempted to grab the meat in its mouth. The actual sequence is variable; sometimes the feeding cheetah simply got up and ran off with its meat. Other times there was a tug of war. In many individual encounters between possessor and competitor for meat, it was possible to identify the cheetahs. Usually it was the larger male that was able to approach a possessor directly without the rear-end presenting and take the meat away. The possessor was usually a smaller individual but would not readily yield. Instead, it swatted and clawed the competitor on the head. All cheetahs fed in sternal recumbency with the meat between but not gripped in their forepaws. Hide was rarely eaten and then only when a small piece was swallowed whole. Fatty tissues were eaten readily but bone was not ingested.

After the summer months, with less traffic there was improved visibility of the approaching meat truck; the cheetahs saw it coming ¼ mile away. They approached the truck and the entrance gate. This posed a security problem since the adjacent section contained hoof stock. The problem was solved at first by the Warden getting out of his jeep with pole in hand and directly confronting the cheetahs while leaving just enough space for the truck to enter the section. The cheetahs also became conditioned to the time of day for feeding and began orienting their vision and movements to the entrance gate at a similar hour every day. The security problem became more acute so the truck entered the exit gate. From where the cheetahs lay up they did not have visual contact with the truck until it was already in the section. Another modification in feeding was to transfer meat from truck to jeep outside the cheetah section then feed directly from the jeep. In a short time cheetahs generalized to all jeeps. All Lion Country jeeps are marked identically, and starting at middawn, the usual feeding time, cheetahs chased jeeps until fed. The chases were short in length if no meat was dropped. They came to discriminate time of day and entrance through the exit gate. The jeeps that were chased most fit into this overall stimulus pattern.

One of the most important releasers in all feeding responses was a cheetah running. Once any cheetah got up and ran, the others in view got up and ran in the same direction.

A reasonably high activity level should stimulate natural conditions and increase the probability of breeding. It is plausible that activity from hunting stimulates production of hormones. We induced activity in many ways, for example by tying a burlap bag on the end of a rope and dragging it behind a fast-moving jeep. The cheetahs chased the bag around the road. Tidbiting away from favored lying-up spots induced running toward the jeep and competitive interactions. The use of recorded cheetah vocalizations played repeatedly over the jeep's loud hailer stimulated approach and inspection but in time there was partial habituation. The use of live prey released more regularly would probably meet a desired level of activity; however, no matter how critical this might be for successful breeding, public pressure and humane laws could prevent it. It is encouraging that the successful breeding program at San Diego Wild Animal Park has involved regular feeding of live prey, and that the public is made aware of it (Herdman, 1972).

The fact that no cheetahs have yet given birth at Lion Country Safari is an indication of the unsuitability of the breeding program. After the assumed stress of transport from South West Africa and introduction and adaptation into an unusual environment, we expected nothing more during the first nine months. Courtship and mating were relatively frequent, as described above and there was only one reproductively mature female present during the period of intense mating. Since the injured female's recovery and return, she was an outcast and this might have affected her mating activity. Of the other four females, all subadults on arrival, only one was courted. San Diego Zoo received five females and though they were all mature there was only one birth during the same study period (R. Herdman, 1973). The greater amount of physical and social space afforded at San Diego, as compared to Lion Country, and the absence of human disturbance, might easily be the factors in breeding success.

Seasonality of mating is possible, as Herdman (1973) predicted in the San Diego cheetahs. It should be kept in mind that if contact and mere proximity of foreign males is a factor in inducing estrus, mixing the cheetahs at Lion Country Safari after a period of separation may have been sexually releasing. Since estrous periods are relatively long in cheetahs, which could be an adaptation to the female's solitary way of life, it is plausible that foreign males have an additional stimulatory effect on an estrous female. In any event, the adult female is an unsociable animal and should be kept isolated until signs of heat appear. This is not done at San Diego Wild Animal Park, and may explain why only one of their ten females has conceived in nearly three years. At World Wildlife Safari we separate males from females except for breeding. At this writing, our cheetahs are still in their first breeding season.

Lion Country Safari has the world's largest collection of cheetahs and keeps them in a relatively small area. The habits of the wild pregnant female lead one to believe that once a female is pregnant there must be some accommodation for allowing her to avoid contact with other cheetahs. There are a number of ways in which this can be done. The pregnant female probably requires an area large enough to be able: to move away from her cubs to feed after they are first born; to move her cubs in the area, for which shrub plantings or artificial platforms can be provided; and to be free of contact of any kind with other cheetahs or fearful stimuli that could induce abandonment of cubs. These provisions would come as close to the female's behavioral requirements as is possible (with also feeding live animals). Cheetahs prefer lying up areas which provide good visibility, and in addition they actively seek out higher elevations, such as dirt mounds, hills, logs, rock piles, from which they view the surrounding landscape. It should be possible for the expectant female to satisfy these apparent needs in the captive environment.

Concerning sex ratios, Lion Country Safari chose the high number of males to attempt to duplicate the natural setting of several males or groups pursuing and courting an estrus female. If several females come into heat at the same time, one group of courting males may not be optimal. Furthermore, there are cases in captivity of several females being in heat at the same time (Herdman, 1973), in which case several groups of males might be an improvement. However, frequency of copulation is low and all adult males, properly fed and in good health, should produce fertile sperm during the breeding season. I would consider two competing males optimal for impregnating a receptive female.

There are many factors which must be considered, and it is difficult to make absolute recommendations. For example, wild cheetahs kept in two adjacent paddocks in Kenya, both with identical ground cover and food, had strikingly different breeding success (W. York, pers. comm.). Litters were born in both areas but survival was higher in the 5-acre than in the 20-acre area. The smaller compound had a mother and her subadult cubs which apparently posed little threat to their mother's second litter. Two litters born in the much larger paddock apparently suffered from high intraspecific predation. The individuals in the latter area were foreigners when enclosed. Owing to the nature of their social relationship cheetahs bred better in the smaller area. Both groups of cheetahs hunted and killed Thomson's gazelle regularly, but most captive breeding programs to date have not carried out live feeding involving high activity in hunting on a routine basis. The limited amount of live feeding is normally kept secret because well-meaning preservationist groups would be highly resistant. Furthermore, enough space combined with an agile, speedy prey would come close to recreating a natural setting.

Of all the Felidae, the cheetah has been the least successful in breeding relative to its numbers in captivity. Obviously cheetahs breed well in the wild. Any cheetah breeding program should strive to duplicate the natural setting initially, and then, with success, experimentally eliminate those conditions or factors that are not essential.

The most successful cheetah breeding to date has been at San Diego (Herdman, 1972, 1973), where a female's second litter is being raised not by hand but entirely by the female. These cubs are killing rabbits and are growing up as cheetahs would in the wild, socialized to cheetahs, not to men, and perfecting predatory skills. They are likely to contribute a third generation when adults, and continued study will lay further groundwork for reintroduction programs in the wild when and if the need arises.

Postscript:

Four cubs were born at World Wildlife Safari on 8 September, 1973, a little more than one year after the cheetahs were imported and placed in the secluded compound. Mating occurred in June shortly after the two males were placed with the female. The mother is caring for the cubs.

13 September, 1973

R. I. E.

⑨ Conservation

The cheetah, fastest of the world's land animals, is racing toward extinction. One or another of man's desires have harassed many species into oblivion, but the cheetah is getting what seems to be special extermination treatment. It is being trapped for its value alive, shot for the value of its fur, poisoned because it supposedly kills livestock, occasionally hunted for "sport," made homeless through the loss of its habitat, and starved through the loss of its prey's habitat. It would be difficult to think of another reason for persecuting these lithesome spotted cats. Certainly they do not threaten man's safety; they have never been known to attack man unless cornered, a situation in which most animals fight back.

The cheetah once was widely distributed throughout most of Africa except in the arid desert and heavy rain forests. It was also common in the Middle East and southern Asia. It is now nearly extinct in Asia and the Middle East, but one population in Asia is increasing in Iran, due to careful protection and management by the Iranian Game Department. It is rare in much of South and North Africa. There may still be remnant populations in West Africa in the area around Kano, Nigeria; in north-central Africa in the vicinity of Fort Lami; and around the southern borders of Lake Chad. The Sudan probably has a respectable number in Bahr El Ghazel Province. Farther east, cheetahs have disappeared from areas of former abundance in Ethiopia and are believed greatly reduced in Somalia. Tom Foose of the

University of Chicago recently returned from a general reconnaissance of Angola. He spent nearly three months in the wildlife preserves of Angola and other countries in southern Africa without seeing a single cheetah. He told me that one warden in Angola remembered seeing only two cheetahs in a decade whereas at one time they were much more common. The only remaining cheetah stronghold outside of East Africa is South West Africa where population trends are not being monitored.

With the exception of the dog, the cheetah shares the longest association of hunting with man; and, like dogs, cheetahs are easily tamed and handled. The early Egyptians used cheetahs for coursing game. They took each new generation from the wild, as cheetahs did not breed in captivity. The constant removal of potentially reproductive animals from populations, along with natural mortality, probably contributed to an early decline of the cheetah in northern Africa. Thousands of cheetahs in Asia were captured and used by the Mongol rulers on their deer-hunting expeditions, according to Marco Polo. The use of hunting cheetahs became a pastime that proved tasteful to European rulers and those of Asia Minor as well. From the courts of the Turkish sultan to the hunting lodges of the German emperor at Vienna, cheetahs were tamed for hunting everywhere after the sixteenth century. The sport of hunting with cheetahs in India reached such proportions that when cheetahs were near extinction early in this century, the supply was maintained with African-caught cheetahs. A demand in Asia for hunting cheetahs still exists. There are some who believe that the Asian race of the cheetah has interbred in some areas with imported African stock. I have no data on this, but hope it is not true.

The demand for wild-caught adult cheetahs is a drain on populations in several ways. For every cheetah trapped, tamed, and trained successfully, several die in the process. If cheetahs were good breeders in captivity, as are lions, for example, they would be much more abundant today. But cheetahs are *not* good breeders in captivity. Even in the wild, breeding can be difficult. Cheetahs, unlike lions and wolves, lack "baby-sitters." The cheetah female raises her young by herself, not in a group of adults that help care for the cubs. If a female lion is killed or removed, her cubs may survive, but orphaned cheetah cubs are doomed.

All young cheetahs exported abroad come from the wild. South West Africa is the only remaining part of the cheetah's once great range in which a supply is available to animal dealers. Poachers in Kenya told me that live cheetahs are worth great sums of money in Ethiopia, which, according to them, is the center for exporting black-market cheetahs to other countries. Somalia has been equally if not more important in the illegal spotted cat trade, but the government is now taking protective action.

Until just recently a demand has been put on younger cheetahs for pets. One has but to visit southern Florida or California to see or hear of so-and-so's cheetah. While I was in Palm Beach recently, I talked with a local veterinarian who told me of the frequent purchases of cheetahs there. He said that many of them die shortly after arriving in this country. His more wealthy clientele simply had them replaced. Until 1972, cheetahs were available in this country from animal dealers for $1500–$2000. In southern California there are many privately owned cheetahs. They are a status symbol, much like owning a leopard or cheetah coat is.

The World Pet Society is made up of many cheetah owners. Though they profess to be striving to breed cheetahs in captivity, most of them are not willing to allow their pets to mate. The group sought my advice on how to increase breeding success, but I found that many of the members were hesitant in placing their cheetahs together in fear that they might injure each other. They seemed to be worried not so much about the health of the cheetahs as about possibly decreased attractiveness due to wounds or scars! For persons who own cheetahs to be more concerned with their individual pet's appearance than with the survival of the species is incredible.

One of the Palm Beach veterinarian's wealthier clients, who had lost two cubs, became interested in supporting research to enable the breeding of cheetahs in captivity. This would help satisfy the demand of zoos and private citizens for live cheetahs and so slow down the trapping of wild cheetahs. More recently the Donner Foundation generously contributed to the cheetah-breeding program of the San Diego Zoo, which is meeting with success.

It was not until 1967 in Rome that a cheetah gave birth to cubs in captivity that did not have to be hand-raised, although cheetahs have given birth in zoos several times. In the unnatural zoo environment mothers often ignore or kill their cubs, but even when they are hand-raised many die. It is desirable to have the mother raise her own cubs. The cubs acquire natural immunities to disease through the mother's milk. Furthermore, the cubs grow up socialized to cheetahs and not to men. Thus when they are sexually mature they are much more likely to mate and properly raise, rather than reject, their own cubs.

I am convinced that the presence of competing males and adequate space for courtship chases is optimal for breeding success. These have been lacking in previous zoo attempts to breed cheetahs. The few isolated successes, for example at Whipsnade Zoo, are best explained as the rare case in which a pair is more tolerant of an unnatural setting. We cannot count on the exceptions, rather we must find formulas which are effective for most cheetahs. Toward this end I have mentioned several males and adequate space—no less than five acres in area. Further, there is reason to believe that females are behaviorally and physiologically more receptive to males when they have been isolated away from the males until they come into heat. For this reason, and the additional fact that this is the case in the wild, males should be kept away from the female until she is in season.

In some species there are indications that hunting behavior is conducive to overall condition as well as to the production of reproductive hormones which may affect breeding success. Therefore, and in keeping with the general principle of duplicating natural conditions, I should recommend that feeding live prey be carried out regularly as one aspect of any breeding program. Unless the keepers of cheetahs are highly skilled in nutrition, it is desirable in any event to feed whole fresh carcasses since this provides proper nutrition and enhances health in captivity. It is heartening that in 1972 the United States Office of Endangered Species (U.S.D.I.) and the professional zoo association (A.A.Z.P.A.) have joined forces in arriving at a set of minimum standards, which will determine whether or not a zoo or park is suited to accept cheetahs for breeding and study.

The breeding programs should naturally be a part of restocking efforts; however, assuming that the restocked habitat is suitable, cheetahs born in captivity must be allowed to acquire the education from their mothers that they would have received in the wild. Even if cheetah cubs are removed from the wild to be restocked later, or for some reason the cubs are removed from their mother, they will in time acquire a normal predatory sequence, as Stevenson-Hamilton discovered years ago in South Africa. Under any circumstances a restocking program should implement live feeding, preferably with the prey species that are abundant in the area to be restocked.

Humane and preservation groups will attempt to prevent this practice in the United States and certainly there could be some opposition in South Africa. My personal belief is that we must place the conservation status of the cheetah and whatever is necessary to achieve it above our displeasure with otherwise inhumane practices in our system of priorities.

There are many well-meaning lay groups, "cat fanciers," etc., which keep cheetahs as pets, and are concerned over their status. However, they are unable to sacrifice the personal, emotionally rewarding contact with their pets (Fig. 9–1), and therefore have little chance to breed them. Their attempts are further complicated by a lack of proper nutrition, space, and understanding of the animals' social needs. I have always wanted to own a pet cheetah, but cannot rationalize private ownership of endangered pets unless captive breeding is successful.

Although there is still a large demand for live cheetahs in zoos and wildlife parks, the picture looks ever brighter in this regard. Lion Country

Figure 9–1 L. Von Heczey, president of the Cheetah Rescue Club, with his pet, Genie.

Safari, World Wildlife Safari, and San Diego Zoo are attempting to breed cheetahs on a large scale. All projects are relatively new, but already San Diego has had success with the births of two litters. In time such efforts as these should prove successful. Similar projects aimed at restocking have been started in South Africa.

The advent of more intensive agriculture in Africa not only has prevented normal animal migrations and movements necessary for maintaining habitat conditions, but also has cost predators their prey. The cheetah in India might have survived had it not been for the loss of grazing land for the blackbuck, the cheetah's major prey.

In South Africa, the decrease of prey with the advent of European development and farming techniques probably contributed as much to the decline of predatory species as did killing the predators themselves. As cheetahs are highly specialized for certain species of prey, a decrease in these species is leading to a decline in cheetahs. The cheetah's status is comparable to that of the wolf in North America, which not only was shot, poisoned, and trapped, but whose prey populations also were decimated.

The cheetah is considered vermin in many areas of Africa for its supposed great threat to sheep, goats, and small calves. However, I observed several cheetahs that regularly hunted on Somali sheep lands, and they showed not the slightest interest in the sheep. The herdsmen told me that they never had trouble with *enduma* though they saw cheetahs daily on their ground. An occasional cheetah may damage livestock, as sometimes occurs with an unusual wolf or coyote; but it was certainly not a common occurrence in Kenya.

Kenya's laws allow, however, that if a cheetah is killed for damaging livestock, it can be sold for its fur. A visitor to Nairobi will notice that the tourist shops are full of cheetah furs—whole, or on wristwatch bands, hatbands, handbags, and so on. These furs come from cheetahs that supposedly attack domestic animals. No steps are taken to establish whether stock losses actually occurred, but the amount seems greatly exaggerated.

One animal dealer catches cheetahs in South West Africa and has supplied a great number to individuals and zoos in this country. His operation is successful because of a loophole clause in the laws protecting the cheetah. This clause states that any cheetah deprecating stock can be killed or live-trapped. The dealer in question has a broad network of connections with local farmers. When they enter a complaint, he live-traps the animal then sells it abroad. The farmer prefers having the cats taken alive because the dealer pays him more than he could get for shooting the cheetah and selling its skin. The sad thing is, of course, that most of the cheetahs are *not* damaging livestock. On the other hand, were it not for a commercial interest these cheetahs would simply be killed outright. The situation and concern for conservation in South West Africa is dreadful, and in the long run, the future of all wildlife there is dubious. Perhaps it is a good thing that the would-be doomed cheetahs are transported to places such as San Diego Zoo and Lion Country where valuable research can be conducted which hopefully will lead to large-scale breeding programs. Current field work indicates that there are probably as many as 3000 cheetahs in South West Africa, apparently the largest extant population in any country (N. Myers, pers. comm.). These new data imply that the few hundred live exports per year may not even drastically affect the population. The great danger is eventual loss of habitat and prey.

A major man-cheetah "agricultural" conflict is brewing. Equatorial Africa has the richest mammalian fauna in the world. In order to preserve the wildlife of Africa in the face of rapid population growth, many biologists have advocated the use of surpluses of natural animal populations for food rather than attempting to replace the wild animals with domestic livestock. It is claimed that more protein may be obtained per acre by cropping the wild fauna than by attempting to raise domesticated cattle.

How will the predators conflict with this so-called "game ranching"? This question is vital to the continued survival of the large predators. The use of wild protein sources may result in a demand for killing large predators. Man will be cropping the wild herds, thereby replacing the natural role of large predators in the community. When men take a predominantly economic concern for meat-producing wildlife, they will regard predators as vermin. Game ranching, if it becomes widespread, may do wonders for preserving the hoofed game, but may be devastating to the predators. Tourists may be the predators' saviors. Visits by tourists will provide additional income to large game ranchers. The ranchers would do a much greater business if predators were present for observation and photography. The special fascination of the carnivores would offset loss of income from predation on hoofed game. Additionally, some game ranchers have found that by charging sport-hunters to kill predators, they more than make up for the losses of game to the predators. On Rhodesian game farms the harvest of carnivores is carefully regulated and managed to produce a sustained yield. This is an excellent innovation since an economic incentive will prevent extermination.

The cheetah survey recorded a mere eight cheetahs known to be poached in East Africa, but certainly poaching has taken a far greater toll. Though it is illegal anywhere in East Africa to kill cheetahs for fur, the demand in the United States and elsewhere for women's garments led to the illegal killing of cheetahs for the black-market fur industry. The U.S. Endangered Species Protection Act does protect the cheetah as of 1972, and the recent moratorium on spotted cat furs by the International Fur Traders Federation is encouraged and long overdue. This should help considerably to ease poacher pressure on cheetahs.

Poachers told me that cheetah furs brought them 50 American dollars in Kenya and that they killed from one to six animals each time they went into northern Kenya after them. The most damaging poachers are European or Asian, as they use firearms and vehicles to run down and kill cheetahs. Because the cheetah inhabits the more open areas, poaching by natives using traps, snares, or primitive weapons is probably not as substantial. Wide-scale poaching for meat, rampant on the edges of many national parks, does result in snaring and killing cheetahs. How many are taken in this way is unknown.

Cheetahs once were hunted in India as game animals. In Africa they have been shot for sport; for example, Teddy Roosevelt related that Kermit killed seven cheetahs in one day—a record. Several safari hunting firms included cheetahs in their bag, and they were taken by most game hunters in South Africa in the latter part of the nineteenth century. The cheetah survey reported only 16 cheetahs shot in East Africa. However, this figure is much too low. It does not, for instance, include those shot by farmers.

Cheetahs are outlawed as game in most African countries today. Furthermore, they are not now considered desirable trophies by most hunters. Therefore, it is doubtful that sport hunting remains an important mortality factor. However, I was appalled on several occasions when speaking with big-game hunters in Africa and America to hear these sportsmen say that they had shot cheetahs illegally while on safari. This is the exception, however, and not the rule.

Man's only hope for holding onto an aesthetically precious part of his environment is to stress the value of *all* wildlife. As in North America, South Africa's once great wildlife legacy now exists only in a few national parks and preserves. The same condition seems likely for East Africa. However, in an unstable political and economic environment, the continuation and wise management of wildlife even in national parks is tenuous (Myers, 1972). Parks such as Serengeti in Tanzania that require small area extensions to make them closed ecosystems, areas that can support wildlife the year round, are not winning any battles. This is so even though tourist visitation continues to increase annually.

An encouraging contribution to the long-term survival of *all* wildlife is the increasing tourism by Europeans and Americans, for example in East Africa. The largest income in Kenya is in the Ministry of Tourism and Wildlife. Although dollar signs cannot be placed on aesthetic values, the economic importance of wildlife in Africa, hopefully, will ensure its survival there. A growing trend in black Africa's recognition of the vital tourism industry is witnessed today in Zambia's international advertising for safari tourism.

Several underdeveloped African countries have failed to recognize the value of their wildlife. Though temporarily experiencing short-term success through overexploitation, they are headed for long-term failure. Somalia, Mozambique, and Angola, to mention a few, have witnessed serious declines in populations of many wildlife species that are attractive to tourists. Though a few game preserves and national parks exist on paper, they are poorly funded and inadequately managed. Walking along a road in the Angolan sanctuary for the greater sable antelope—a magnificent but endangered species—Tom Foose found eight leopard traps within a distance of only five miles! Preserves and national parks can be managed properly and more than pay their own operational expenses.

The International Union for the Conservation of Nature and Natural Resources (IUCN) recently has established a Cat Specialist Group in their Survival Service Commission. The group held its first meeting at the International Symposium on Ecology, Behavior, and Conservation of the World's Cats in March 1971 (Eaton, 1973b). Lion Country Safari, National Parks and Conservation Association, and the World Wildlife Fund sponsored the symposium. The meeting was the first worldwide step toward conserving the cheetah and other felines. The unanimous resolution of the attending scientists and 40 conservation groups was to urge the federal government to "back up the efforts of state governments in banning the importation and sales of skins and products from the wild cats of any country of the world." Early in 1972, the United States Department of Interior placed the cheetah and seven other wild cats on the list of endangered species. The scientific community had considerable influence in this unprecedented legislation, which hopefully will lead other countries into banning importation of cheetah hides.

The IUCN has given top priority to the cheetah and leopard in Africa, and field studies to determine the status and population trends of cheetahs in several areas are under way. The IUCN and the World Wildlife Fund, both in Morges, Switzerland, depend on donations from private individuals and organizations to carry out these and other needed surveys of endangered wildlife species. The sooner the funds required to conduct field surveys materialize, the sooner steps can be instituted to preserve threatened cats. Oddly enough the cheetah and leopard studies are being sponsored by the International Fur Traders Federation. A second international conference on the world's cats met in March, 1973, sponsored by World Wildlife Safari and the Institute for the Study and Conservation of Endangered Species (ISCES). Emphasis was on reproductive biology and management for captive breeding. These and other meetings will collect and disseminate new information valuable to breeding programs for the cheetah and other problem breeders.

Several things need to be done immediately if we are to stop the decline of cheetahs, to ensure their continued survival, and hopefully, to see them reintroduced in their former ranges;

(1) Encourage the practice of successful breeding of the many presently captive cheetahs. This would provide a source of cats for zoos and private individuals. Eventually it would permit the restocking of cheetahs where they are now extinct or may become so.

(2) Discourage illegal killing and sale of cheetah fur under the guise of stock damage by encouraging the African nations to employ government trappers on a complaint basis for removing and relocating any cheetahs that are really causing damage. Or an effective system of compensating farmers and graziers losing livestock might be established.

(3) Encourage African governments to extend national parks to make them closed ecosystems so as to prevent prey and their predators from leaving the parks and becoming susceptible to poaching.

(4) Encourage women all over the world to stop buying products made from cheetah and spotted cat skins.

(5) Encourage other nations to declare a moratorium on spotted cat furs.

The largest single threat to all wildlife, not only cheetah, is the expanding human population. As people require more land for living space and food, less land will remain to support wildlife. Even if man can survive under more densely populated conditions, the quality of his life will deteriorate as wild animals disappear. Wild places and creatures are important to man. They show us that there is more to life and the universe than our own selfish concerns.

Bibliography

Adamson, J., 1969. The spotted sphinx. Harcourt, Brace and World, New York.

Ardrey, R., 1962. African genesis. Collins, London.

Asdell, S., 1964. Patterns of mammalian reproduction. Cornell University Press, Ithaca, New York.

Bourliere, F., 1954. The natural history of mammals. Knopf, New York.

Bourliere, F., 1963. Specific feeding habits of African carnivores. *African Wild Life*, **17**(1):21–27.

Brown, J., 1964. The evolution of diversity in avian territorial systems. *Wilson Bull.*, **76**:160–169.

Burt, W., 1943. Territoriality and home range concepts as applied to mammals. *J. Mammal*, **24**:2.

Burton, M., 1962. Systematic dictionary of mammals of the world. Museum Press, London.

Crandall L. S., 1964. Management of wild animals in captivity. University Chicago Press.

Darling, F., 1960. An ecological reconnaissance of the Mara Plains in Kenya Colony. *Wildlife Monograph*, No. 5.

Dart, R., 1964. The ecology of the South African man-apes. In: D. Davis (Ed.) Ecological Studies in Southern Africa. W. Junk, The Hague.

Deevy, E. S., Jr., 1947. Life tables for natural populations of animals. *Quart. Rev. Biol.*, **22**:283–314.

Denis, A., 1964. Cats of the world. Constable and Company. London.

De Vore, I. and S. L. Washburn, 1963. Baboon ecology. Pp. 335–367, In: F. C. Howell and F. Bourlieve (Ed.'s) African ecology and human evolution.

Downs, J. F., 1948. Domestication: an examination of the changing relationships between man and animals. *Kroeber Anthro. Soc. Papers* 22.

Eaton, R. L., 1969 a. Cooperative hunting behavior between cheetah and jackal and a theory of domestication of the dog. *Mammalia*, **31**(1):57–62.

Eaton, R. L., 1969 b. The social life of the cheetah. *Animals*, **12**(4):172–175.

Eaton, R. L., 1970 a. The hunting behavior of the cheetah. *J. Wildl. Mgmt.*, **34**(1):56–67.

Eaton, R. L., 1970 b. Group interactions, spacing and territoriality in cheetah. *Zeitschrift für Tierpsychologie*, **27**(4):481–491.

Eaton, R. L., 1970 c. The predatory sequence with emphasis on killing behavior and its ontogeny, in the cheetah. *Zeitschrift für Tierpsychologie*, **27**(4):492–504.

Eaton, R. L., 1970 d. Notes on the reproductive biology of the cheetah. *Int. Zoo. Yb.*, **10**:86–90.

Eaton, R. L., W. York and W. Dredge, 1970. Lion Country Safari and its role in conservation, education and research. *Int. Zoo. Yb.*, **10**:215–216.

Eaton, R. L., 1973. Aggressive behavior in the lion. Ph.D. Thesis. Purdue University, Lafayette, Ind.

Eaton, R. L. and S. J. Craig, 1973 a. Reproductive biology and captive management of the cheetah. In: *The World's Cats*, I. Ecology and Conservation, R. L. Eaton (Ed.). World Wildlife Safari and Institute for the Study and Conservation of Endangered Species, Winston, Oregon.

Eaton, R. L. (Ed.), 1973 b. *The World's Cats*, I. Ecology and Conservation. World Wildlife Safari and Institute for the Study and Conservation of Endangered Species, Winston, Oregon.

Eloff, F., 1973. Ecology and social behavior of the Kalahari lion. In: *The World's Cats*, I. Ecology and Conservation R. L. Eaton (Ed.). World Wildlife Safari and Institute for the Study and Conservation of Endangered Species, Winston, Oregon.

Encke, W., 1960. Birth and rearing of cheetahs at Krefeld zoo. *Int. Zoo. Yb.*, **1**:85–86.

Errington, P. L., 1946. Predation and vertebrate populations. *Quart. Rev. Biol.*, **21**(2):144–177; (3):221–245.

Errington, P. L., 1963. Muskrat populations. Iowa State University Press, Ames.

Estes, R. D., 1967. Predators and scavengers. *Nat. Hist.*, **76**(2):20–29; **76**(3):38–47.

Estes, R. and J. Goddard, 1967. Prey selection and hunting behavior of the African wild dog. *J. Wildl. Mgmt.*, **31**(1):52–70.

Etkin, W. and D. G. Freedman. Social behavior from fish to man. Phoenix Books, University Chicago Press.

Ewer, R. F., 1971. Maternal care in the Felidae. Paper presented at First International Symposium on Ecology, Behavior and Conservation of World's Cats March 15–17. Laguna Hills, California.

Firouz, E., 1971. Conservation and wildlife management in Iran. Game and Fish Dep't., Iran.

Flower, S. S., 1931. Contributions to our knowledge of the duration of life in vertebrate animals. V. Mammals. *Proc. Zool. Soc.* London, **100**:145–234.

Flower, W. H. and R. Lydekker, 1891. An introduction to the study of mammals: living and extinct.

Florio, P. and L. Spinelli, 1967. Successful breeding of a cheetah in a private zoo. *Int. Zoo. Yb.*, **7**:150–152.

Foster, J. B., 1966. The giraffe of Nairobi National Park. *E. African Wildl. J.*, **4**:139–148.

Foster, J. and D. Kearney, 1967. Nairobi National Park game census, 1966. *E. Afr. Wildl. J.*, **5**:112–120.

Graham, A., 1966. Cheetah survey. *E. African Wildl. J.*, **4**:50–55.

Graham, A. and I. Parker, 1965. East African Wild Life Society cheetah survey. 20 pp. (Mimeo).

Guggisberg, S., 1963. Simba. Howard Timmins, Capetown.

Herdman, R., 1972. Captive cheetah reproduction. *Zoonooz.* **40**(10):4–12.

Herdman, R., 1973. Cheetah breeding program. In: *The World's Cats*, I. Ecology and Conservation, R. L. Eaton (Ed.). World Wildlife Safari and Institute for the Study and Conservation of Endangered Species, Winston, Oregon.

Holling, C. S., 1961. Principles of insect predation. *Ann. Rev. Entomol.*, **6**:163–182.

Hopwood, A. T., 1951. The Olduvai fauna. Pp. 20–25, In: L.B.S. Leakey (Ed.). Olduvai Gorge: a report on the evolution of the hand axe culture in beds I–IV., 160 pp.

Horn, H., 1966. The measurement of overlap in ecological studies. *Am. Nat.* **100**:611–617.

Hornocker, M., 1969. Winter territoriality in mountain lions. *J. Wildl. Mgmt.*, **33**:457–464.

Hornocker, M., 1970. Predation on deer and elk by mountain lion in the Idaho primitive area. *Wildl. Monogr.*, 21.

Klopfer, P. H., 1964. Behavioral aspects of ecology. Prentice-Hall, New Jersey.

Kruuk, H., 1972. The spotted hyena. University Chicago Press.

Kruuk, H. and M. Turner, 1967. Comparative notes on predation by lion, leopard, cheetah and wild dog in the Serengeti area, East Africa. *Mammalia*, **31**:1–27.

Kühme, W., 1966. Beobachtungen zur Soziologie des Löwen in der Serengeti-Steppe Ostafrikas. *Zeit. Saugetierk.*, **31**(3):205–213.

Lack, D., 1954. The natural regulation of animal numbers. Clarendon Press, Oxford.

Lambrecht, F. L., 1966. Some principles of tsetse control and land-use with emphasis on wildlife husbandry. *E. African Wildl. J.*, **4**:89–98.

Lamprey, H., 1963. Ecological separation of large mammal species of the Tarangire Game Reserve, Tanganyika. *E. African Wildl. J.*, **1**:63–92.

Laws, R. M., 1966. Age criteria for the African elephant. *E. African Wildl. J.*, **4**(1).

Leyhausen, P., 1956. Verhaltensstudien an Katzen. Paul Parey, Berlin.

Leyhausen, P., 1965. Uber die Funktion der relativen Stimmungshiérarchie. *Zeitschrift für Tierpsychologie*, **22**(4):412–494.

Leyhausen, P. and R. Wolff, 1959. Das Revier einer Hauskatze. *Zeitschrift für Tierpsychologie*, **16**(6):666–670.

Lorenz, K., 1966. On Aggression. Methuen, London.

Mac Donald, M., 1966. Treasure of Kenya. G. P. Putnam's Sons, New York.

McLaughlin, R., 1970. Aspects of the biology of cheetahs, *Acinonyx jubatus* (Schreber) in Nairobi National Park. M. Sc. Thesis, University of Nairobi, Kenya.

Mech, D. L., 1966. The wolves of Isle Royale. U. S. National Park Service, Fauna Series 7, Washington, D. C.

Mech, D. L., 1970. The wolf. Nat. Hist. Press, New York.

Meggitt, M. J., 1961. The association between Australian aborigines and dingoes. In: H. Leeds and P. Vayda (Ed's.). *Man, Culture and Animals*. A.A.A.S. 78, Washington, D. C. 304 pp.

Manton, V. J. A. 1970. Breeding cheetahs at Whipsnade Park. *Int. Zoo Yb.* **10**:85–86.

Meinertzhagen, R., 1938. Some weights and measurements of large mammals. *Proc. Zool. Soc. London*, **108**:433–439.

Mercier, A., 1961. Our friend Yambo. Souvenier Press.

Mitchell, B. L., J. B. Shenton and J. C. M. Uys, 1965. Predation on large mammals in the Kafue National Park, Zambia. *Zool. Africana*, **1**(2):297–318.

Montagu, A., 1942. On the origin of the domestication of the dog. *Science 96* (2483).

Muckenhirn, N. and J. F. Eisenberg, 1973. Predation and spacing behavior in the Ceylon leopard. In: *The World's Cats*, I. Ecology and Conservation, R. L. Eaton (Ed.). World Wildlife Safari and Institute for the Study and Conservation of Endangered Species, Winston, Oregon.

Murie, A., 1944. The wolves of Mt. McKinley. U. S. National Park Service Fauna Series 5. Washington, D. C.

Murray, M., 1967. The pathology of some diseases found in wild animals in East Africa. *E. African Wildl. J.*, **5**:37–45.

Murray, M., H. Campbell and W. H. F. Jarrett, 1968. *Spriocersa lupi* in a cheetah. *E. African Wildl. J.*

Myers, N., 1972. The long African day. McMillan, New York.

Petrides, G., 1965. Advisory report on wildlife and national parks in Nigeria. *Amer. Comm. for Int. Wild Life Protection, Special Publication*, **18**:48.

Petrides, G., 1956. Big game densities and range carrying capacity in East Africa. *Trans. N. Amer. Wild. Conf.*, **21**:525–537.

Pienaar, U. de V., 1969. Predator-prey relations amongst the larger mammals of the Kruger National Park. *Koedoe*, **12**:108–176.

Pimlott, D. H., 1967. Wolf predation and ungulate populations. *Amer. Zool.*, **7**:267–278.

Rabb, G. B., J. Woolpy and B. E. Ginsburg, 1967. Social relationships in wolves. *Am. Zool.*, **7**:305–311.

Rasmussen, D. I., 1941. Biotic communities of the Kaibab plateau. *Ecol. Monogr.*, **3**:229–275.

Rausch, R., 1967. Some aspects of the population ecology of wolves, Alaska. *Amer. Zool.*, **7**:253–265.

Roberts, W., 1951. The mammals of South Africa. Trustees of the mammals of South Africa.

Robinette, W., J. Gashwiler and O. W. Morris, 1961. Notes on cougar productivity and life history. *J. Mammal.*, **42**:204–217.

Roosevelt, T. and E. Heller, 1922. Life histories of African game animals, I. John Murray, London.

Rosenzweig. M. L. and R. H. MacArthur, 1963. Graphical representation and stability conditions of predator-prey interactions. *Amer. Nat.*, **97**:209–223.

Schaller, G. B., 1963. The mountain gorilla, ecology and behavior. University of Chicago Press, Chicago.

Schaller, G. B., 1966. Progress report of Serengeti lion study. *E. African Wildl. Soc. Newsletter*, November.

Schaller, G. B., 1967. The deer and the tiger. University Chicago Press.

Schaller, G. B., 1968. Hunting behavior of the cheetah in the Serengeti National Park. *E. African Wildl. J.*, **6**:95–100.

Schaller, G. B., 1972. The Serengeti lion. Univ. Chicago Press.

Schenkel, R., 1967. Submission: its features and function in the wolf and dog. *Am. Zoologist*, **7**:319–329.

Scott, T. G., 1943. Some food coactions of the northern plains red fox. *Ecol. Monogr.*, **13**:427–479.

Scott, J. P. and J. L. Fuller, 1965. Genetics and social behavior of the dog. Univ. Chicago Press, Chicago.

Shortridge, G. C., 1934. The mammals of South West Africa, I. W. Heinemann, London.

Slobodkin, L. B., 1963. The growth and regulation of animal population. Holt, Rinehart and Winston, New York.

Slobodkin, L. B., F. E. Smith and N. G. Hairston, 1967. Regulation in terrestrial ecosystems, and the implied balance of nature. *Amer. Nat.*, **101**(918):109–124.

Spinelli, P. and L. Spinelli. 1968. Second successful breeding of cheetahs in a private zoo. *Int. Zoo Yb.*, **8**:76–78.

Sterndale, R. A., 1884. Natural history of the mammals of India and Ceylon. Thacker, Spink and Company, Calcutta.

Stevenson-Hamilton, J., 1947. Wild life in South Africa. Cassel, London.

Stewart, D. R. M. and J. Stewart, 1963. Status and distribution of the mammals of Kenya. Coryndon Museum, Nairobi.

Stewart, D. R. M. and L. M. Talbot, 1962. Serengeti survey. *Africana*, **1**:24–27.

Talbot, L. M. and M. Talbot, 1963. The wildebeeste in Western Masailand, East Africa. *Wildl. Monogr.*, **12**:60 pp.

Thompson, R. In press. The cheetah in captivity. In: R. L. Eaton (Ed.). The World's Cats, Vol. II.

Van de Weaken, 1968. Preliminary report on cheetahs in zoos and in Africa, *Zool. Garten* **35**(3):156–61.

Varaday, D. 1966. Gara Yaka's Domain. Collins, London.

Vesey-Fitzgerald, F. 1960. Grazing succession in East African mammals. *J. Mammal.*

Walther, F. Mit horn and hoof. Paul Parey, Berlin.

Walther, F. R., 1969. Flight behavior and avoidance of predators in Thomson's gazelle. *Behaviour*, **34**(3):184–221.

Wendt, H., 1959. Out of Noah's ark. Houghton Mifflin Company, Boston.

Woolpy, J., 1968. Social organization of wolves. *Natural History*, **72**:46–55.

Woolpy, J. and B. Ginsburg. 1967. Wolf socialization: a study of temperament in a wild social species. *Am. Zool.* **7**:357–364.

Wright, B. S., 1960. Predation on big game in East Africa. *J. Wildl. Mgmt.*, **24**(1):1–15.

Wyman, J., 1967. The jackals of the Serengeti. *Animals*, **10**:79–83.

York, W., 1973. Pharmacological restraint of felids. In: The World's Cats, Vol. I. Ecology and Conservation, R. L. Eaton (Ed.). World Wildlife Safari and Institute for the Study and Conservation of Endangered Species, Winston, Oregon.

Young, E., 1967. Nutrition of wild South African felines and some viverrids. *African Wildl.*, **21**(1).

Zeuner, F. E., 1954. The domestication of animals, pp. 327–352. In: E. Singer (Ed.) A history of technoligie, I. Clarendon Press, Oxford.

Adamson, Joy, 2, 22, 27, 31, 32, 36, 37, 39, 40, 41
Ardrey, R., 3
Asdell, S., 47

Bourliere, F., 19, 24, 49, 50, 51, 55, 67, 68, 81, 97
Brown, J., 98
Burton, M., 17, 25, 46

Craig, S. J., 109, 112, 147
Crandall, L. S., 17, 18, 30, 37, 46, 133

Darling, F., 50
Dart, R., 3, 86
Denis, A., 16, 17, 25, 32, 129, 133
DeVore, I., 56
Downs, J. F., 86
Driver, P. M., 67

Eaton, R. L., 15, 35, 53, 96, 135, 147
Eisenberg, J. F., 51
Eloff, F., 44, 50, 51, 141, 144
Encke, W., 32, 37, 133
Errington, P. L., 50, 96
Estes, R. D., 4, 50, 55, 65, 67, 130
Etkin, W., 3

Firouz, E., 19
Florio, P., 32
Flower, W. H., 17, 18, 22
Foster, J., 10, 11, 30, 32, 51, 58, 67
Foster, J. B., 30, 95
Freedman, D. G., 3
Fuller, J. L., 86

Ginsburg, B. E., 86
Goddard, J., 4, 50
Graham, A., 19, 25, 27, 28, 30, 32, 39, 40, 41, 44, 45, 46, 47, 48, 51, 52, 56, 57, 65, 129, 143
Guggisberg, S., 50, 67

Herdman, R., 32, 34, 40, 42, 44, 113, 117, 118, 153, 154
Hopwood, A. T., 16
Horn, H., 81
Hornhocker, M., 46, 51
Humphries, D. A., 67

Kearney, D., 11, 51, 58, 67
Kruuk, H., 50, 51, 55, 56, 57, 62, 65, 67, 68, 69, 134
Kühme, W., 50

Lack, D., 35
Lambrecht, F. L., 5
Lamprey, H. F., 25, 26, 57
Leyhausen, P., 99, 130, 132, 142, 143
Lorenz, K., 3, 95, 97
Lydekker, R., 17, 18, 21, 22

MacDonald, M., 19
McLaughlin, R., 11, 29, 30, 31, 32, 40, 45, 53
Manton, V. J. A., 32
Mech, David L., 3, 4
Meggitt, M. J., 86
Meinertzhagen, R., 19
Mercier, A., 37
Mitchell, B. L., 66
Montagu, A., 86
Morris, O. W., 41

Subject Index